DIGITAL TRANSFORMATION BEGINS
WITH **DEVICE** TRANSFORMATION

Digital Transformers

SRINIVAS KUMAR

FOREWORD BY

ALBERTO YEPEZ AND **BRIAN NUGENT**

ISBN: 978-1-09837-019-0

DIGITAL TRANSFORMERS

The journey to digital transformation begins with a change in mindset as the top line, and the courage to step outside the comfort zone as the bottom line.

Dedicated to, and in fond memory of, my parents who taught me that honest, industrious and selfless duty is life's mission and is all that matters in the end.

To the Mocana Engineering Team:

You cannot hire a dream team.

You have to build one.

Then they help you build the dream.

Preface

The theory and practice of cybersecurity requires an intricate understanding of the cyber anatomy that includes machines, software, user psychology, hacker mentality, corporate policies and processes, interworking protocols, and the network fabric where the crown jewels of informational and operational systems reside.

The Internet era enabled rapid globalization and created a worldwide market for products and services. Cyber is the fiber of global commerce. The Cyber era is on the cusp of opening up a global market for cybersecurity services in a wide array of industries from finance, healthcare, infrastructure, manufacturing, transportation, to customer devices and the Internet of Things (IoT). The tectonic plates for the services industry are shifting from network management to managed security services for business continuity in a compromised environment.

From small, medium and large enterprises to consumers, the FUD (Fear, Uncertainty and Doubt) factor weighs in heavily as cyber-enabled systems govern daily regime from automobiles, smartphones, laptops, tablets, data centers, and manufacturing equipment to household appliances. The cybercrime syndicate has emerged as a formidable adversary and poses a serious challenge as critical digital assets and business processes are vulnerable to theft of intellectual property, invasion of privacy, and orchestrated subterfuge. Leveraging dual-purpose technology (such as encrypted communications, and anonymization), a sophisticated arsenal of malware toolkits, and programming talent, hackers have succeeded in staging coordinated high profile attacks penetrating modern perimeter and endpoint defenses.

Security cannot be an afterthought anymore as borders are history and threats are ubiquitous. The battle lines have been drawn between the hackers and the tacklers, with a call for action and proportional response. Establishing trust and resiliency in the titanic vastness of cyberspace requires rethinking the security paradigm and continuous vigilance. Resilient defense against a powerful cybercrime syndicate requires a paradigm shift in enterprise risk management. This necessitates a holistic solution to aggregate 360-degree assessments and provide a structure and calculus to create a consolidated statement for real-time, actionable decision making and control. Establishing a synergy between policy, process and technologies, to measure the runtime operational integrity of systems, requires a force multiplier that augments the human-in-the-loop with an automation based expert system for evidence analysis and incident response. Timely observations need instrumentation to correlate data and context for protection at the epicenter of data breaches – the soft core.

In the theological realm, trust may be unconditional and based on implicit faith. However, in the cyber realm, distrust is implicit and, trust is always conditional and based on explicit verification. The influence of cyber on daily activities at work and home behooves a higher level of vigilance and savviness from netizens, and throughout the supply chain, in this cyber era.

Even as the world economy has transitioned through a simple needs-based adaptation over the centuries from agricultural, industrial, and financial to a services economy, the interdependencies between people, process and machinery has remained intricate. The thin line between products and services is rapidly vanishing as advances in technology reduce the half-life of mainstream products and sustaining services grow into the qualitative differentiator. Threat intelligence provides a frictionless surface for cyber resilience, and an effective defense strategy requires a paradigm shift from a "need to know" to "need to share" mindset.

Cyberspace has the potential to challenge and influence the social and political order across the globe, as witnessed by polarized and uncivil national elections, the Arab spring in the Middle East, and the tea party movement in the United States. Wars that were historically fought with battalions of soldiers, guns and mortars are fought today with satellite technology, unmanned drones and precision guided missiles that cost billions of dollars. The future wars may be fought with a geo-distributed pack of hacktivists with a benign or malicious purpose, at a low cost of operation funded by nation states or syndicates, with a highly reduced risk of casualties, friendly fire, or collateral damage as in traditional wars. From ransomware for blackmail, to stirring chaos amongst citizenry, to advanced coordinated attacks on critical infrastructure to challenge the establishment or disruption of financial services, to initiating political upheaval for ideological reforms, cyberspace provides opportunities for the motivated.

There are no decisive or war-ending victories on the cyberspace battlefield. The cybercrime industry is omnipresent, outside and inside the perimeter defenses, and expansive. The return on investment in cybercrime is staggering. The first strike capability of an attacker to stage a preemptive attack and survive without any retaliation action poses an enormous risk and is a lucrative financial incentive. In the decades ahead, reconnaissance and data exfiltration techniques of unmanned and precision guided malware will pose a daunting challenge to the gate keepers of critical assets and intellectual property. The monetization of threat intelligence and post breach forensic investigations lures the security industry away from grass roots technology innovations to deal with the resilience of systems, rationality of processes and culpability of people. Advances in dual-use technologies have outpaced the evolution of trustworthy systems, processes and users.

Digital Transformation is the coming wave in globalization without borders. Much as the Internet, cloud, and smartphones have transformed economies worldwide, the emerging tsunami of devices in activities of daily living at home and work will bring forth amazing conveniences and tragic consequences. A zero-trust model for digital (re)engineering requires collaboration, rather than competition, between silicon chip manufacturers, device manufacturers, operating systems, security protocols, application developers, cloud platform providers and cloud services. Since the summer of 2016, the investors, executives and engineers at Mocana Corporation embarked on this journey of value creation to protect the future of "things". A solution architecture was formulated working closely with the ecosystem of silicon chip manufacturers, device vendors, original equipment manufacturers (OEMs) and service providers. The effort extended to factoring in fit-and-finish for deployment and operations, dovetailing with time honored workflows, retrofitting legacy brownfield devices and manufacture at scale of greenfield devices. While the work is not over by any stretch of imagination, we hope it has at least inspired a wave of innovation in the industry. This book is our sincere effort to share and empower architects everywhere to join us in this journey to define standards and specifications to achieve the objective of building trust in the wilderness of cyberspace.

Foreword

It was imminent from the early days of Mocana in 2002, that this was the beginning of a long journey in securing cyberspace as the new frontier. At that time, the Internet was barely 12 years old, not yet in its teens!

Mocana's mission was to establish cryptography as the tool and weaponize devices for tamper resistance and resilience against cyber-attacks by nation state actors and cybercrime syndicates. Towards this goal, our initial objective was to develop a platform for security by design. That journey culminated with the implementation of a security stack to execute trusted applications on untrusted platforms. In the summer of 2016, with the onset of silicon based secure elements as root-of-trust anchors the tectonic plates had shifted. We embarked on our next objective to develop a trusted operations platform for smart devices. The Internet of Things (IoT) wave that was emerging needed protection controls for safety and cybersecurity. The relentless cyber-attacks and data breaches over the past decade warranted rethinking by all stakeholders from silicon vendors to device manufacturers and operators. The limitations of detection and prevention-based technologies had to be overcome with an architecture that provided resilience, protection, and trustworthiness.

Mocana's long-term partnerships with major silicon vendors and device manufacturers, and the collaborative effort, established a solid framework based on standards to harden legacy brownfield and greenfield devices at scale. As the promises of artificial intelligence (AI), machine learning (ML), 5G, and edge cloud technologies come to fruition in the years ahead, CISOs, CIOs, CTOs and product security architects will require embedded trust in devices and a horizontal IoT platform. To achieve synergetic confluence of information technology (IT) and operational technology (OT), vast investments will be required in all sectors – manufacturing, healthcare, transportation, defense, public utilities, retail, entertainment, networking, printing, and residential. Such a large-scale changeup will indeed begin a revolution in digital transformation.

A committed Mocana team of cybersecurity, embedded systems, and cloud services architects persevered for four years and developed a services and device platform to address the serious challenges that lay ahead for a diverse set of purpose-built OT/IoT devices in the wilderness of cyberspace. These platforms lend themselves to non-disruptive and synergetic integration with security operations centers (SOCs), device management systems, and application management systems. The solution empowers line of business applications to secure data and communications without reengineering, provides original device manufacturers (ODMs) a fast path to achieve compliance, managed security service providers (MSSPs) a SaaS based revenue stream, and cloud platform vendors trusted operational and device intelligence to prime analytics engines for subscription-based risk management services.

With operational efficiencies and reduced operational expenses for device owners and operators, subscription-based revenues for both managed security service providers and cloud platform providers, Mocana's IoT platform for embedded trust is on course to revolutionize digital transformation in the years ahead. Our journey started with the Internet boom and will continue with the Digital Transformation boom, until cyberspace is protected for future generations to continue on this voyage.

—Alberto Yepez, Brian Nugent
March 2021

Acknowledgements

Mocana's IoT platform for embedded trust epitomizes the determined and tireless effort of an incredible product development and solution engineering team at Mocana. The crew of this mission are duly credited below, in alphabetical order, for their priceless contributions in transforming a vision into a solution.

- Atul Gupta
- Bruno Hernandez Esquivel
- Colton Willey
- Hedy Ying-Chong Leung
- Jaime Haletky
- Kimberly Banow
- Lou Sanchez-Chopitea
- Mahendra Shelke
- Payton Schwarz
- Pramod Malibiradar
- Rajendra Prasad Kandukuri
- Ruslan Ulanov
- Shashank Pandhare
- Shrey Tandel
- Shreya Uchil
- Srikesh Srinivas

We extend our sincere appreciation to the sales, marketing and business development team at Mocana, through the formative years, for their relentless trust in the core engineering team and in the power of technological innovations that drive enduring change.

- Bill Diotte
- Dave Smith
- Emily Miller
- Jeanne Pardo
- Jon Mills
- Najib Khouri-Haddad
- Tim McAllister

We extend our sincere gratitude to our esteemed board members and investors for the opportunity and for funding the research and development effort. The path of "innovation without disruption" requires persistence and tenacity to stay on the trail.

- Alberto Yepez, *Co-Founder & Managing Director, ForgePoint Capital*
- Brian Nugent, *Founding General Partner, Sway Ventures*
- John Scull, *Co-Founder & Managing Director, Southern Cross Venture Partners*
- Rob Coneybeer, *Co-Founder & Managing Director, Shasta Ventures*

My Special Thanks To:

Atul Gupta for his leadership in designing and delivering the core development and operations platforms, services APIs, and for meticulous 24/7 customer satisfaction.

Bruno Esquivel for his perseverance and remarkable contributions to our cryptographic capabilities, hardware acceleration operators, and the secure transport stack.

Colton Willey for his excellence and spirited contributions to our cryptographic capabilities, cryptographic abstraction platform, hardware acceleration platform, performance optimizations, and device protection for RTOS and Mac/OS platforms.

Hedy Leung for her excellence and remarkable role in driving quality assurance and verification to render timely product releases, the foundational platform for device protection, to our customers.

Jaime Haletky for his inspiration leadership role as our cryptographer-in-chief, delivering above and beyond expectations on classical and post-quantum ciphers, the cryptographic abstraction platform, the hardware acceleration platform, and performance optimizations for resource constrained platforms.

Kimberly Banow for her outstanding contributions and valuable suggestions, as our technical writer-in-chief, to improve all aspects of our extensive product documentation, user guides, and operator manuals.

Lou Sanchez-Chopitea for his enthusiastic contributions and brilliance in build and test automation for the core development and operations platforms.

Mahendra Shelke for his astute leadership in designing and delivering an elegant and scalable device monitoring and analytics platform.

Payton Schwarz for his energetic and outstanding contributions to our cryptographic capabilities, hardware acceleration operators, APIs, connectors for migration from open source, and the secure transport stack.

Pramod Malibiradar for his grit and extraordinary contributions to extend and enhance the capabilities of the secure transport stack, connectors for migration from open source, and the trust abstraction platform.

Rajendra Prasad Kandukuri for his immense expertise and extraordinary impact on extending device protection and the core development platform to RTOS platforms, support for secure elements, and outstanding integration and troubleshooting guidance to customers.

Ruslan Ulanov for his enormous and priceless contribution to the design and evolution of the operations platform, user experience, services APIs, and the orchestration services architecture.

Shashank Pandhare for his incredible follow-the-sun leadership and accomplishments that enriched the core trust abstraction platform and the operations platform for device protection, and for rendering timely and quality global customer support services.

Shrey Tandel for his can-do attitude, self-motivation and remarkable contributions to our cryptographic capabilities, cryptographic abstraction platforms, hardware acceleration operators, connectors for migration from open source, and the secure transport stack.

Shreya Uchil for her huge help and generous patience in proofreading and providing thoughtful feedback on my unrelenting blog posts and whitepapers. Her live(ly) and engrossing workshops exemplify the power of Mocana's technology and use cases to device vendors, service providers, and device operators.

Srikesh Srinivas for his energetic and outstanding contributions to device monitoring, operations platform robustness, scripting and APIs, in stealth mode, as the youngest and profoundly valuable member of our core team.

Joel Don for his meticulous graphics and artistic icons featured on my blogs, whitepapers, presentations, and in this book.

Ken Black, Sherry Black and Andreas Wolf for their steadfast support and outstanding contributions to multi-factor verified boot, tamper resistance content delivery, scripting, and leadership in driving FIPS certification of the core cryptographic engine.

Jon Mills, Tim McAllister and Emily Miller for their endless faith in the technology and engineering team, can-do attitude, self-motivation and relentless commitment to the cause of innovation.

Dave Smith, Jeanne Pardo and Bill Diotte for being the pillars of optimism, and their iron resolve, complete confidence, and constant encouragement.

"Nothing vast enters the life of mortals without a curse"

— Sophocles

Navigating Through the Book

The subject matter of cybersecurity, confluence of information technology (IT) and operational technology (OT), and digital transformation is vast to grasp. The book has therefore been purposefully structured as chapters.

Chapters 1 & 2 outline the urgency for embedded cyber protection on devices and why cybersecurity is still elusive after two decades of innovation building multi-layer defenses around devices.

Chapter 3 describes the chronological evolution of things – systems, solutions and trust models.

Chapter 4 proposes a way forward beyond detection and prevention to protection, the tools and methods, drivers, benefits and challenges.

Chapter 5 describes the essentials for passage from IT to OT ecosystems, to implement digital transformation.

Chapter 6 explains industry specific strategies required to mitigate risks, and countermeasures to harden workflows and processes.

Chapter 7 describes the elements of trust required in the cloud to empower digital transformation.

Chapter 8 reveals the status quo in digital transformation projects and findings from a global market survey to solicit views from key stakeholders and security professionals in the field of OT and IT.

Chapter 9 describes a foundational framework and architecture to serve as the building blocks for device transformation.

Chapter 10 uncovers the upstream risks and exploits in the supply chain.

Chapter 11 describes the conundrums of trust models from the perspective of IT, cloud, OT and digital transformation.

Chapter 12 proposes a risk model, in contrast to traditional threat models, for device protection with tamper resistance and operational resilience.

Chapter 13 underscores the decisions required on the uphill road and climb to achieve desired OT-IT convergence.

Chapter 14 provides a perspective about why breaches (continue to) happen.

Chapter 15 emphasizes why examination of signaling integrity and data exchanges is imperative for device protection.

Chapter 16 summarizes approaches to inspect runtime operational integrity.

Chapter 17 reflects on the IT journey through the intricacies and challenges of security controls, towards achieving the objective of a unified workflow and single pane of glass for OT-IT convergence.

Chapter 18, the last chapter in this voyage, brings to focus the intricacies of threat vectors, risk assessments, attacker modeling, defensive tools and methods to establish trust in devices and secure the epicenter of cloud computing.

Table of Contents

Chapter 1

Protecting the Digital Planet

During the cold war, a new weapon was built to pierce any shield and for every new weapon a new shield was built that could not be pierced. This is the infinite game theory about will and resources, and who exhausts one or the other first and drops out of the game.

In terms of cybersecurity, I have been pondering the infinite game concept for over a decade and through multiple startup ventures in this space. We have continued to design "shields and weapons" like intrusion detection engines and anomaly detection powered by threat intelligence, rules grammar, regular expressions, probability theory, deductive, inductive and abductive reasoning. Yet, despite all this, the industry is still exposed to high-profile data breaches and ransomware. What are we missing? That is the question. Perhaps the answer is that we may be solving the wrong problem.

When it comes to cybersecurity for the Internet of Things (IoT), we need to examine not just where the problem lies today but also, and more importantly, where it may manifest again tomorrow. The 5G network and cloud at the edge are poised to be radical game changers in our lives. What we are observing today is far beyond digital transformation and data brokers. Google is no longer about a search engine, but about APIs. Facebook is no longer about faces, but about data. Microsoft is no longer about an operating system, but about a cloud platform. Cars are no longer about miles per gallon, but about software defined transportation. Factories are no longer about automation for production at scale, but about artificial intelligence (AI) and machine learning (ML) for robotization. Data centers are no longer about big data clouds, but about edge compute and software defined storage down in the fog.

What we are observing is the power of transformation. From the stone age, through the middle age, modern age, digital age, to the data age – the global economy has evolved to the digital platform of data as the fuel that drives intelligence. Intelligence can transform knowledge into tools to be creative, or knowledge into weapons to be destructive. To begin to solve our cybersecurity challenges, we can harvest device intelligence for use as a self-defending tool for cyber protection. Likewise, we can transform device lifecycle management into protection lifecycle management. And finally, enhance privacy and integrity of data to establish trustworthiness of data to prevent weaponization.

The tectonic plates are moving in cyber space. The Future of Things is in the "Things of the Future". Things are no longer connected simply by wires and protocols, but by waves (5G) and APIs. These "Things of the Future" are devices with north, south, east, west connectivity, requiring a perimeter-free, friction-less operating surface.

The traditional information technology cyber security rules identify indicators of compromise on a hacked device – as a forensic science. Forensic science is the discipline in which professionals use scientific means to analyze physical crime evidence. Life science is the study of life and living things. A paradigm shift is required to enable data sciences to new heights and objectives for a safer digital planet. The new IoT cyber protection paradigm must use artificial intelligence with device intelligence – as a life science. As we transition from old security models, cyber strategies will necessarily pivot from reactive methods such as detection, forensics, and forensic science, to proactive methods such as protection (vaccination), self-defense (immunity), and a life-science approach to cybersecurity.

Cyber Protection as a Service is the enabler to protect IoT platforms in the era of digital transformation. Ask not whether the device is compromised, ask whether the device has protection. Change the Rules. Protecting emerging IoT devices and edge clouds is an Infinite Game, and it has just begun.

Here is a fascinating lesson about protection lifecycle, that history is testimony of, that remarkable solutions are possible with ingenuity.

The Ashoka Stupa, a 7-meter-long pillar outside Delhi, India, was built 1600 years ago and is made of iron that has not rusted. It is 98% iron and the remaining 2% comprises of lead, brass, bell metal (copper and tin) and phosphorous from wooden blast furnaces (instead of modern limestone blast furnaces). It does rust in the first phase with water and air (ferrous oxide FE-O), however a chemical reaction between the metal and the first phase creates misawite to form a ferrous oxide hydroxide (FeOOH) which forms a passive layer of "self-defending protection".

(https://en.wikipedia.org/wiki/Iron_pillar_of_Delhi)

Figure 1: Ashoka Stupa

Chapter 2

Why Cybersecurity is Still Elusive

Over a decade ago, we were told the cloud was not just a "secure" cloud, it was a "trusted" cloud. Today, cybersecurity companies are still playing detectives and cloud platform vendors and service providers are acquiring them for billions of dollars. In the end, can we trust chief risk officers to do the right thing and invest in protection after they have exhausted all detection alternatives? While detection is a valuable and necessary forensic analysis tool, not including protection as a strategy in the digital tool chest is a fatal oversight. Protection is what you do before detection becomes a necessity.

Adopting new approaches is a matter of "willingness" to change and the "ability" to handle change. It requires both. Willingness is the belief that unless we do something different, the outcome will not change. You are focused on changing the outcome (the bull's eye) with a different approach. Ability is a matter of cost – capital and operational expenses, and whether the expenses are justified – recoverable through sales or mandated by regulatory compliance to stay in the game. When either the willingness or ability is lacking, status quo and quick fixes win in the heated battle of wits.

Why is it that security is such a liability to pay for? Fundamentally, end users (consumers) don't understand the consequences. A lost, stolen or damaged device is all end users care about. Whether the device is trustworthy is just not in the calculus. Are you watching the shows on your television or is the television watching you? Is your neighbor, a stranger sitting next to you, your smart ride driver, or a hacker listening to your conversations? Are home security systems monitoring intruders or you and your family? Is loss of privacy the price of security? Or should you protect both your privacy and your data? Consumers expect their device vendors to protect them from becoming victims, just like car seats for infants and air bags for adults regulated by insurance policies. Continuing to play detectives is like waiting on victims to perform forensic analysis on, to serve as a warning to future potential victims. It does not address the root cause that protection is a womb to tomb supply chain mindset. Regulations in cybersecurity have been structured to be vendor friendly, and not consumer friendly.

As device vendors and service providers embrace the emerging opportunities of 5G to widen the data pipes into your home and work, and edge computing to bring computing to your neighborhood, perhaps it is time to ponder. This is also the age of the Smart Consumer, who pays for "daily value" of goods and not "cost" of goods. The major changes in our lives over the past two decades have been driven by entertainment media, mobile smart phones and cloud services. The "ability" challenge is the consumer's out of pocket costs. Consumers want fair pricing – not promotional discounts, which is where pay-for-use usage-based billing rather than device-based billing is the winning value proposition. You pay for the service you choose to use, whether it is an advanced feature, a compliance checkmark, or a premium service that is valuable to you in your line of business. This is where protection becomes a service play and not something any device vendor can afford to absorb upfront as a value-added-tax. The device vendors and device owners/operators are victims of cyberattacks and cannot be expected to pay for the crime.

One broker in the middle, between device vendors and device owners/operators, is the managed security services provider with the detection toolkit. Another broker required is the protection service provider with the platform to offer cyber protection as a service, that includes a chain of trust that begins with the manufacturer and persists through the supply chain of providers and publishers of content to the device. A tamper-resistant self-defending posture establishes a state of trust. This trusted state must then be preserved with protection controls to reject content with tamper-evidence and measured for proof of trustworthiness. In quantum physics, entangled particles remain connected – so actions performed on one affect the other even when separated by great distances. Albert Einstein called it "spooky action at a distance". If content entangled with a device is tampered anywhere along the supply route, the device is tampered. So, to make the device tamper-resistant, one has to protect against spooky actions at a distance.

For vendors of cybersecurity solutions, it is not about taking on competition – the only competitors here are the hackers who will always be one step ahead in this game – but about building a "security task force" with an arsenal of weapons to take on the enemy that is disrupting our daily lives. As Einstein famously said – the questions have not changed, but the answers have. The risks have not changed, but the consequences have.

Chapter 3

Evolution of Things

The evolution from Enterprise IT to outsourced IT, cloud silos, and field OT has transformed solutions, systems, trust, and things, to start the wave of digital transformation. The paradigm shift from centralized and distributed to connected is the emerging reality of things.

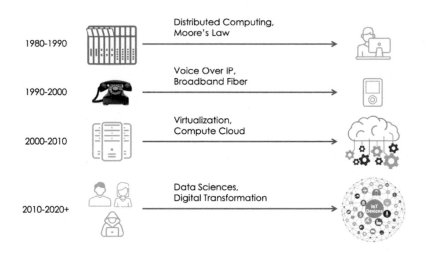

Figure 2: Evolution of Things

Evolution of Solutions

The chronological sequence of transformation in solutions was as follows:

1) Bring Users to the Network

2) Bring Your Own Device

3) Bring Applications to the Cloud

4) Bring Services to the Cloud

5) Bring Cloud Services to the Device

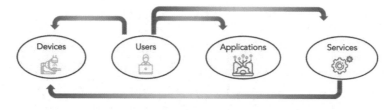

Figure 3: Evolution of Solutions

Evolution of Systems

The evolution of systems was the ripple effect of the evolution of solutions.

1) Centralized Compute Platforms

2) Digital Communications (Internet)

3) Cloud Computing (Virtualization, Platform as a Service)

4) Applications and Services (Software as a Service)

5) Data Sciences (Artificial Intelligence, Machine Learning)

6) Actionable Intelligence (Totality of Evidence, Contextual Relevance, Timeliness for Remediation)

Evolution of Trust

The tightly coupled systems in the enclaved corporate networking fabric, or wiring closet, evolved into loosely coupled systems and perimeters began to dissolve, leading to a perimeterless network. The evolution of trust was the consequence of security concerns instigated by the evolution of loosely coupled systems.

1) Identity of Users (Interactive, Multi-Factor) for Authentication

2) Encryption of Data for Communications over Insecure Media

3) Integrity of Data over Unreliable Media

4) Confidentiality of Transactions in the Cloud (User to Service)

5) Authentication of Devices for Device Management Services

6) Integrity of Autonomous Messages (Device to Device)

7) Supply Chain Provenance (Heterogeneous Components)

chip maker   OEM   device owner   service provider   connected devices

Figure 4: Evolution of Trust

Connectivity of Trusted Things

The connected ecosystem of machine to machine, device to edge gateway, and edge to cloud requires identification and authentication mechanism with a brokerless (scalable) zero-trust model with immutable identity and root of trust anchors.

1) Things managed manually by human operators

- Edge Systems

- Gateways, Access Points, etc.

2) Things that connect to other Things over closed non-IP networks (Buses, Serial Links)

- Integrated Mission Systems

- SCADA Stations & Controllers, Aviation FADECs, Engine Control Units, etc.

3) Things that connect to Things over open IP networks

- Autonomous Systems
- Vehicle to Vehicle, Unmanned Aerial Vehicle, Telematics Control Units, Satellite to Ground Station, Ground Station to Air Systems, etc.

Usability of Trusted Things

The trust factor is a function of the Root of Trust anchor (hardware, firmware, virtual or software) on the device and permissioned enrollment into a circle of trust. Trust is a state and requires persistence of the trusted state, with tamper resistance across the supply chain (from manufacture to distribution, deployment and in-field maintenance) and resilience built into the device. The big data challenge in the IT *upstream* ecosystem, on-premise and in the cloud, may be attributed to the volume, velocity and variety of data. In the OT *downstream* ecosystem, the challenge is in the operational, administrative, maintenance and provisioning functions of field devices.

1) Volume of Assets and Critical Artifacts

- Number of devices
- Number of keys
- Number of certificates

2) Velocity of Protective Maneuvers

- Transfer of ownership
- Frequency of key rotation
- Frequency of certificate renewal

3) Variety of Protection Controls

- Key types
- Key strength
- Key usage

Artifact Type	Strength of Protection		
	Low	Medium	High
Passwords	Embedded in Application Factory Defaults	Encrypted Node Locked No Factory Defaults	Known Only to Authorized Users Multi Factor Authentication
Keys	Password Protected Stored on File System	Password Protected Encrypted Node Locked	Protected by Secure Element
Key Usage (Signing)	Persisted in Memory	Key Rotation (Pre Configured)	Secure Enclave (Intel SGX, Arm TZ)
Key Usage (Encryption)	Persisted in Memory	Dynamic (Negotiated by Protocol Handshake) Ephemeral (Session, Temporary) Key Rotation (Pre Configured)	Secure Enclave (Intel SGX, Arm TZ)
Certificate Issuer	Self-Signed	Enterprise Certificate Authority	Commercial Certificate Authority
Root of Trust Certificate	Issued by Device Owner (Post Market)	Issued by Device Vendor (Pre Market)	Provided by Secure Element
Device/Application Certificates	Unprotected Stored on File System	Encrypted Node Locked	

Figure 5: Strength of Protection (Passwords, Keys and Certificates)

The Fast ID Online (FIDO) alliance promotes open standards for strong authentication methods. The bane of factory default passwords must be overcome with Root of Trust anchors embedded in headless devices for trusted interconnect.

The IoT SAFE (SIM Applet For Secure End-2-End Communication) standard provides device manufacturers and IoT service providers the ability to leverage an integrated SIM (iSIM) as a Root of Trust for secure provisioning of cryptographic artifacts to protect data at-rest and in-transit for privacy and confidentiality.

The Promise of Digital Transformation

The promise of digital transformation is the synergetic fusion of data sciences and connected devices based on the power of artificial intelligence (AI) and machine learning (ML) to reduce operating expenses through efficiencies in manufacturing, distribution, operations and maintenance. The notion of trust requires the benefits of digital transformation to embody privacy and confidentiality as an intrinsic element of data sharing. Data is the new currency and the wheels of a digitally transformed economy will be powered by sharing of device intelligence to prime upstream and downstream AI/ML engines.

- ➡ Artificial Intelligence
- ➡ Machine Learning
- ➡ Operational Efficiency
- ➡ Digital Privacy
- ➡ Data Protection
- ➡ Data Sharing (Owner, Broker, Merchant)

Figure 6: The Promise of Digital Transformation

Chapter 4

The Way Forward

The multi-layer defense model fundamentally comprises of three strategies – detection, prevention and protection. The associated tools, methods, drivers, benefits and challenges determine adoption and effectiveness.

Tools and Methods

Detection	Prevention	Protection
1) Device Discovery (Profiling) 2) Vulnerability Assessments (Passive Scans) 3) Threat Intelligence (CVEs, Expressions, Reputation Lists, Signatures, IOCs) 4) Events & Logs (SIEM, SOAR)	1) Network Traffic Monitoring (Deep Packet Inspection) 2) Image Introspection 3) Anomaly Detection (Deviation from Baseline) 4) Threat Intelligence 5) Network Segmentation 6) Quarantine Device 7) Manual Remediation	1) Tamper Resistance (Self Defending) 2) Supply Chain Provenance (Trust) 3) Secure Cryptographic Enclaves 4) Condition Based Maintenance (AI/ML) 5) Remote Device Recovery

Drivers

Detection	Prevention	Protection
1) Visibility 2) Single Pane of Glass 3) Eliminate Blind Spots	1) Control 2) Forensic Evidence	1) Operational Efficiencies 2) Unified Workflow for Operators (Brownfield & Greenfield Devices) 3) Device Vendor Brand Reputation

Benefits

Detection	Prevention	Protection
1) Unified Asset Management (Enterprise, BYOD) 2) Achieves Compliance	1) Avoids Business Disruption 2) Reduces Cost of Damage	1) Reduces Operation Expenses 2) Avoids Service Outages 3) Scalability (Scale Out)

Challenges

Detection	Prevention	Protection
1) Timely, Relevant & Contextual Threat Intelligence 2) 24/7 Vigilance of SOC Operators	1) False Positives Consume NOC/SOC Cycles 2) True Negatives	1) Requires Agent(s) on Devices 2) Integration with Secure Elements 3) Partnership with Device Vendors

The Ecosystem of Trust

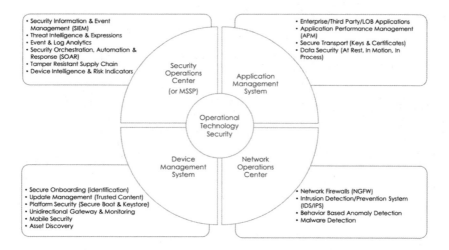

Figure 7: The Ecosystem of Trust

14

The Unified OT-IT Workflow

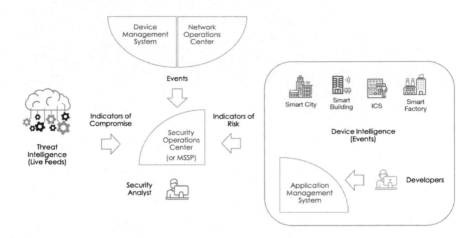

Figure 8: The Unified OT-IT Workflow

Chapter 5

The Passage to Digital Transformation

Device transformation and protection is required to revolutionize digital transformation, just as virtualization and software defined networking were required to revolutionize data centers. Operations Technology (OT) and Information Technology (IT) are fundamentally dissimilar. To begin with, the problem space is radically different – unprotected devices versus gullible users as the carbon. This demands a different solution strategy. Cyber criminals exploit user psychology and over the past decade have truly transformed hacking from a cottage industry to a fine art. A device has no emotions. Devices can be made smarter than humans in cyberspace. Bridging the IT-OT divide (in some cases, a thin line) is the implementation challenge. Even a multi-layer defense strategy is not effective in OT realm. In the IT realm, users are siloed behind the business demilitarized zone (DMZ) and access line of business applications, internal systems, and external services. In sharp contrast, field operators dealing with Industrial IoT (IIoT) must traverse the business, plant, and control DMZ to access internal production systems (e.g. HMI workstations, controllers, robots, and sensors). Further, many autonomous systems in the IoT realm fall outside the line of sight (and scope) of traditional managed IT. Another twist in this tale is that managing authentication directories, PKI infrastructure build-out, key and certificate management services pose implementation challenges for OT operators not well-versed in the myriad of associated security protocols.

Cyber-attacks of the future will be designed to strike high value targets such as critical infrastructure, mass market services and utilities. As the manufacturing, public utility, transportation, healthcare, retail, cloud services, gig economy and defense sectors gradually increase their reliance on the Internet of Things (IoT), lack of serious consideration to building resilience will inevitably lead to tragic consequences in an unprotected ecosystem of inter-connected things. Harvested threat intelligence that drives IT security today is predominantly about how malware successfully evades IT security watchdogs and tricks the end-user into clicking on the poisoned payload to land and expand. OT is about an integrated "womb to tomb" mindset and system for life cycle management – processes, policies and technology. Chasing malware, for behavior fingerprinting, anomaly detection, and regular expressions using sandboxes and honeypots, is a race that cannot be won. Therefore, "zero-damage" protection is better than "zero-day" detection. The real nightmares and challenges in the IT world are the lateral attacks staged within the danger zone. In the world of OT, this is extremely difficult to secure in a fabric without perimeters. The "endpoint" must be transformed into the "protection point".

The serious challenges and risks OT stakeholders face today may be summarized as follows:

- Service Outage or Disruption
- Scalability at Volume of IoT Devices
- Lack of Embedded Security Countermeasures
- Non-Compliance with Standards for Mission Critical IoT
- Proliferation of Connected Devices in the Wild
- Plurality of Platforms (Real Time Operating Systems, Processors)
- Threat Intelligence Hard to Harvest, Absence of Logs (Data Historian)
- Diversity of Device Profiles
- Device is the Weak Link in the Kill Chain

- No Measurements Based Controls for Risk Mitigation or Device Recovery
- No Visibility into Runtime Operational Integrity
- Gaps in Configuration and Change Management (Hard to Detect Anomalies)
- Monitoring Headless Devices
- Malicious Actor in Supply Chain
- Scaling Device Monitoring and Analytics
- Managing Risks. Don't Chase Constantly Evolving Threats.
- Increasing Immunity and Operational Efficiencies
- Attack and Staging Surfaces Radically Different in IT versus OT
- Resource Constraints
- Process Weaknesses
- Plugging Gaps in Security Controls for Compliance

Against the backdrop of these OT challenges and risks, the characteristics of traditional IT centric security solutions may be summarized as follows:

- Controls Purpose-Built for Detection
- Mass Market Solution for Managed IT Infrastructures
- Rip-and-Replace with Next Generation of Antivirus, Host Based Intrusion Detection, Sandboxes, Log Analysis, Behavior Analytics, and Anomaly Detection
- Malware Centric Mindset (More Fish, More Bait – Unscalable)
- User is the Weak Link in the Kill Chain
- Follows the Kill Chain
- Reactive Engine (Detect, Patch, Repeat)
- Sustenance of IT Systems Under Constant Bombardment by Cyber Crime Syndicate

- Operating System (OS) Affinity – Malware Exploits OS Vulnerabilities
- Threat Intelligence without Attribution
- Relies on Well-Known Indicators of Compromise
- Pivots on Malware Signatures, Regular Expressions for Behaviors, and Blacklists
- Forensics Based
- Designed for User Devices (Windows, Linux)
- No Safeguards to Preempt Insider Threats
- Leverages Cloud Based Services for Threat Detection
- Based on a Threat Model
- Malware Morphs Faster than Threats can be Harvested by Honeypots and Sandboxes
- Malware is Localized on Device (Landed Threats)
- Detection Methods are Resource Intensive on Device

Clearly, there is no synergy between the challenges and risks that OT stakeholders face today and the characteristics of traditional IT-centric security solutions to strategically retrofit into OT. The characteristics required for effective next generation OT-centric security solutions may be summarized as follows:

- Controls Purpose-Built for Protection
- Proactive Engine (Trust, Protect, Measure)
- Mass Market Solution for IoT Field Deployment
- Empowers Emerging 5G and Edge Cloud Services
- Builds on a Trust Chain (Root of Trust Anchor)
- Protection for Brownfield and Greenfield Devices
- Tamper-Resistant Content Delivery

- OS Agnostic, Real Time Operating Systems and Enterprise Operating Systems
- Trusted Runtime Integrity Measurements
- Relies on Attested Integrity of the Platform
- Protection of Supply Chain and Device Lifecycle
- Key Protection and Rotation for Embedded Devices
- Protections to Preempt Insider Threats
- Based on a Risk Model (versus a Threat Model)
- Immune to Malware Stains
- Data Diode the Device (Block Unsolicited Communications)
- Protections for Resource Constrained Devices (Messaging Integrity)
- No Factory Default Passwords

The passage to digital transformation in entrenched silos compromising of legacy brownfield and emerging greenfield devices will require device transformation as a strategy for change. Traditional IT network-based countermeasures and malware detection toolkits are inadequate to protect OT devices. The IT security paradigm is to inspect users' access to dynamic general-purpose content posted on external websites and seemingly benign downloads from unknown and unreliable sources. The OT protection paradigm needs to examine purpose-built content delivered to devices through the supply chain by known and implicitly trusted sources. OT will require effective lightweight protection countermeasures on the device for cost and operational efficiencies.

Chapter 6

The Elixir of Things

The challenges, blockers to change, and the decisions required to embark on change vary across industry sectors. The policies and processes that have been engrained over decades of information technology (IT) dominance and stewardship may become the inhibitors of change without a strategy for change. The intrinsic nature of risks has changed and therefore the solutions must too.

Embracing digital transformation will require hardening the workflow and operations, and not clinging hopefully to out-of-date and cumbersome platform hardening guidelines. Security is not a point solution; it is a holistic chain – and it is only as strong as the weakest link in that chain. The effectiveness of security (from soft core to hard edge) requires baked-in controls; not bolted-on controls. The economics of security lies in multi-vendor collaboration as a forethought and not multi-vendor competition as an after-thought. The induction of modern controls must be strategic, measured and rational. Imminent risks have no term limits.

Strategy by Industry Sector

Process Automation

The major risks to process control and automation stems from three factors. The first factor is the diversity of communications methods and industrial protocols that are fundamentally open and insecure, because they were designed to operate within an implicitly secure silo. The second factor is the network firewalls and intrusion detection systems retrofitted into an interconnected and layered ecosystem they were not purpose-designed or intended for operations technology (OT). The third factor is that unlike the IT approach of quarantining infected user workstations (endpoints) with virtual LAN (VLAN) based network segmentation, process control systems in OT are live and quarantining devices in an interconnected system disrupts service and causes undesirable outage. Reactive approaches based on network-based anomaly detection and deep-packet inspection of application protocols will be challenged eventually by the onset of encrypted network traffic (without application reengineering) in the years ahead.

The strategy will require at least: (a) securing the integrity of signaling between systems; (b) managing the digital secrets that offer such security countermeasures – passwords and keys; (c) rotating the digital secrets using X.509 certificates for trusted delivery as a mitigation strategy for recovery on compromise; (d) tamper-resistant content delivery through the supply chain; (e) remote device recovery on compromise with trusted software and configuration updates, and automated key renewal; and (f) auditability for visibility and measurement of compliance posture.

Transportation

The major risks to ground transportation systems stems from the mobile nature of automotive systems. The electronic control units, telemetric/transmission control units, speed control units, onboard diagnostics, navigation systems and consoles will require periodic software and configuration updates. The autonomous operations in modern automobiles will require high assurance of tamper-resistance in inter and intra-system real-time messaging. Isolation of vehicular and entertainment functions will be vital.

The strategy will require at least: (a) securing the integrity of inter and intra-system messaging; (b) securing the digital secrets (keys) that offer such security countermeasures; (c) rotating the digital secrets at scale and as a remote maintenance activity – as a mitigation strategy for recovery on theft or recall; and (d) tamper-resistant content delivery through the supply chain.

Aviation

The major risks to the aviation industry are very broad and stem from the complexity of managing the supply chain, outdated delivery methods, and the criticality of fault tolerance in safety-centric airborne systems. While some of the risks that apply to ground transportation systems are also applicable to avionics, the significant differences are due to the sheer complexity of electronic platforms onboard and implications related to insurance. The willingness and ability to invest and innovate with new technologies is deeply lacking.

The strategy will require at least: (a) securing the onboard messaging systems; (b) securing the digital secrets (keys) that offer such security countermeasures at a nation-state level of alertness; (c) rotating the digital secrets at scale and as a remote maintenance activity – as a mitigation strategy for vulnerability countermeasures; (d) using X.509 digital certificates for key lifecycle management from a secure facility to meet a high level of assurance; (e) tamper-resistant content delivery through the supply chain for traceability; and (f) historic audit trail for trackability of change ledgers.

Healthcare

The healthcare industry is the most complicated environment to secure – as it takes a village – from the medical devices community, to healthcare providers, healthcare workers and government bureaucrats. This is the industry at highest risk because of the sheer volume of unmanaged or hard-to-manage devices and the consequences (life-or-death nature of the trade). The emerging nature of IoT devices and cybersecurity compliance requirements in the healthcare sector requires both equipment vendors and service providers to implement security policies that address the risks posed by cyber-attacks and insider threats. Mission critical production systems and medical devices require protection from unauthorized software updates or configuration changes, and secure authentication of field and remote operators. Legacy enterprise IT managed systems rely on password policies, multi-factor authentication and role based physical and network access. Such controls are inadequate against zero-day cyber-attacks on headless IoT devices that subvert threat intelligence-based intrusion and/or anomaly detection systems designed to prevent data breaches. Therefore, IoT solutions in the healthcare sector require a tamper-resistant system that provides built-in protection controls, trustworthy change management and continuous integrity verification – for high scalability and availability.

The strategy will require at least: (a) securing the identity and integrity of medical devices at the grassroots level; (b) securing the integrity of data exchanges from devices to receivers (display stations and monitors); (c) securing the digital secrets (keys and certificates) on the devices and receivers; (d) rotating the digital secrets at scale and as a managed maintenance activity – for device lifecycle management and transfer of ownership (e.g. remote patient monitoring platforms); and (e) tamper-resistant content delivery through the supply chain for traceability.

Media and Entertainment

The media and entertainment industry are as close to home as it gets. The set top boxes, broadband routers, and 5G gateways are at your doorstep. The implications of data privacy and protection for the consumer are paramount here given the nature of home surveillance systems and information gathering that occurs here. For the business, the major risks are loss of revenue from clones, piracy and theft of bandwidth, and flight of intellectual property. In a competitive marketplace with online stores for home-based entertainment platforms, this industry is poised to stream content and containerized applications to edge cloud platforms. This raises the bar for data privacy and protection at higher data rates, and trusted data for artificial intelligence and analytics at the backend.

The strategy will require at least: (a) securing the on-premise equipment; (b) securing the digital secrets (keys) that offer such security countermeasures;

(c) rotating the digital secrets at scale and as a remote maintenance activity – as a mitigation strategy for tamper-resistance; (d) using X.509 digital certificates for key lifecycle management from a secure facility for effective licensing; and (e) tamper-resistant content delivery through the supply chain for traceability.

Defense

The battlefield on the ground, in the air, on and under water relies heavily on cyberspace and is increasingly becoming a digital ecosystem over radio waves. Tamper-resistance is required at the device, inter-device, and networked systems level for mission critical operations. The major risks stem from the complexity of managing the supply chain (defense contractors), the sophisticated tools and methods in the arsenal of nation-state adversaries, and the air-gapped nature of combat systems. The willingness and ability to invest and innovate with new technologies face budgetary constraints and the effort to integrate for timely field deployment. Further, the paranoia of integrating technologies sourced from the open-source community, new vendors (outside the established supply chain) and technology startups increases the cost and timeliness to build a solution.

The strategy will require at least: (a) using industry standards-based specifications (e.g. NIST, FIPS) vetted for robustness against nation-state attacks; (b) integrating protective countermeasures on devices through the supply chain of equipment manufacturers; (c) managing digital secrets at scale and as a local or remote maintenance activity – as a function of mission control; (d) using X.509 digital certificates for key lifecycle management from a trusted facility; (e) ubiquity across heterogeneous devices and systems for interoperability; (f) tamper-resistant content delivery through the supply chain for traceability; and (g) minimizing personnel re-training to operate the hardened devices and systems on the battlefield.

Printing

The conventional printers for paper documents are evolving in the era of additive manufacturing and 3D printing. The major risks stem from inadequate supply chain protection and theft of intellectual property.

The strategy will require at least: (a) securing the computer aided design (CAD) file delivery with authentication of source and authorization by the publisher; (b) embedding protection to prevent theft of intellectual property (CAD files); (c) extending tamper-resistant protection across the supply chain from the developer to the publisher; (d) protecting containerized applications for workload isolation and key protection in additive manufacturing; and (e) securing the integrity of lateral data transport for interoperability – to deliver technical data in connected digital manufacturing equipment.

Telecommunications and Networking

The wide area network (WAN) and broadband providers will be required to provide IoT connectivity to onboard and service millions of IoT devices and end-point platforms. The device-to-cloud, multi-access edge compute, and cloud-at-the-edge architectures will require trusted connectivity through big data pipelines (secure encrypted tunnels). The emerging 5G network and edge gateways will further increase demand for WAN bandwidth. The incumbent networking equipment vendors will face compliance challenges in the fabric of the edge cloud to meet data privacy and protection requirements.

The strategy will require at least: (a) tamper-resistant edge protection; (b) secure encrypted data transport; (c) key protection and rotation with a hardware-based root-of-trust anchor (e.g. TPM, SIM); and (d) protective counter-measures in the perimeter-less ecosystem against nation-state attacks on mission critical public and national security infrastructures.

Energy

The energy infrastructure, in need of grid modernization, is a high value target for cyber warfare. The major risks to the energy grid stem from five factors. The first factor is physical access to heavily instrumented systems with no protection points on the board at manufacture, and the large attack surface due to the number of access points. The second factor is the manipulation of demand attacks from appliances that can leverage botnets to manipulate the power demand in the grid, to trigger local power outages and potentially large-scale blackouts. The third factor is the targeting of unprotected supervisory control and data acquisition (SCADA) systems and other industrial control system (ICS) software. The fourth factor is that intrusion detection systems are tuned down to reduce the number of false positive alerts, to the point that it becomes useless. The fifth factor is that unlike the IT approach of quarantining infected user workstations (endpoints) with virtual LAN (VLAN) based network segmentation, power generation and distribution systems in OT are live and quarantining devices in an interconnected system disrupts service and causes undesirable outage. Reactive approaches based on network-based anomaly detection and deep-packet inspection of application protocols will be challenged eventually by the onset of encrypted network traffic (without application reengineering) in the years ahead.

The strategy will require at least: (a) securing the integrity of signaling between systems; (b) managing the digital secrets that offer such security countermeasures – passwords and keys; (c) rotating the digital secrets using X.509 certificates for trusted delivery as a mitigation strategy for recovery on compromise; (d) tamper-resistant content delivery through the supply chain; (e) remote device recovery on compromise with trusted software and configuration updates, and automated key renewal; (f) embedded network access controls for perimeter-less defense; and (g) auditability for visibility and measurement of compliance posture – to avoid punitive fines for violations (e.g. NERC-CIP).

Who Benefits?

When the story ends, the device owner and operator live happily ever after. However, this needs to be a win-win for a collaborative strategy to manage cyber risks across the IoT industry. This supply chain begins in the fabrication lab of the semiconductor (chipset) vendor with a root-of-trust anchor (the secure element). The original equipment manufacturer (OEM) or original device manufacturer (ODM) must then integrate a root-of-trust anchor on the equipment (mezzanine board) as a contract manufacturer for the device vendors. The system integrator may then assemble hardened subsystem components from a plurality of device vendors for the specialized IoT industry. Finally, a device operator manages the operations, administration, maintenance and provisioning services. With the advent of software-as-a-service (SaaS) utility models for capital and operational expense reduction, cybersecurity services for IoT devices will inevitably migrate to public, private, or community cloud-based IoT platforms. The passage from on-premise to on-cloud, and the adoption gap between the mainstream device vendors and the managed security service providers, needs to be bridged with a holistic cyber risk management platform that enables digital transformation in the IoT industry.

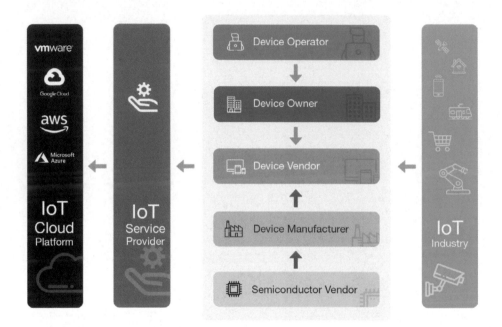

Figure 9: The IoT Ecosystem

Semiconductor Vendor

- Adoption of hardware-based root-of-trust anchors (e.g. TPM, EPID, SIM)

- Enable root-of-trust service with a trust abstraction platform to build ubiquitous device drivers

- Drive device identification and authentication based on an endorsement key and certificate for the root-of-trust anchor

Device Manufacturer

- Born tough devices
- Contract manufacturing of factory hardened devices for tamper-proofing and anti-cloning
- Bolt-on hardware-based discrete root-of-trust anchor
- No factory-default passwords (protected device configuration)

Device Vendor

- Contract manufacturer configures and hardens devices at factory, as per protection profile
- Activate and provision the hardware-based root-of-trust
- Issue birth certificate to license device
- Track and count on-shelf and licensed inventory
- Revoke device certificate to cancel license
- Provision services and application post device onboarding and transfer of ownership for intellectual property protection

Device Owner/Operator

- No cloud platform or service provider lock-in
- Buy protection instead of build-it-yourself with engineering and certification cycles
- Protect brownfield silos without application reengineering
- Ensure interoperability of greenfield and brownfield connected devices for digital transformation of infrastructure
- Eliminate the steep costs and operational complexity of PKI build-out
- Data privacy and protection for mission critical applications with cryptographic key management
- Increase operational efficiency and integrity

IoT Service Provider

- Offer cyber protection as a service to device operators as a utility model
- Drive revenues in the emerging 5G network and edge cloud (smart cities, smart factories, smart factories, smart energy, smart transportation)
- Authenticated device onboarding, updates with supply chain protection, risk monitoring and reports
- Usage based billing with subscription-based level of protection

IoT Cloud Platform

- Offer a high availability platform for IoT service providers
- Marketplace for cyber protection services
- Drive revenues with usage-based billing for compute, network, and storage resources

The elixir to cure cybersecurity risks in IoT will require a prolonged and tenacious commitment to change. The rebirth of the Internet needs to be protection centric and must not relegate security initiatives to an IoT cottage industry in the wild that must defend against sophisticated cyber criminals and nation-state actors with reactive tactics. The transformative and economic potential of IoT requires both a microscopic and telescopic vision of cybersecurity. This has serious implications for cyber insurance companies as well. The willingness of the insurer to pay-off cyber criminals as a mitigation process for recovery of services and compromised devices will only encourage cyber-attackers – not discourage the cybercrime syndicate. If government regulators fail to rise to the occasion and protect cyber commerce and data, the insurance companies will have to step up with guidelines for cyber resilience or suffer from the consequences of attacks on cyber infrastructure. Staying in the infinite game of cybersecurity, against a determined cyber adversary, requires the will and resources of all players in the supply chain.

Chapter 7

The Connected Cloud of Things

The proliferation of autonomous digital devices in our daily lives, what we refer to as the Internet of Things, is poised to connect with other things in a chain of clouds to serve a much larger purpose and make possible a much wider spectrum of services. You can think of this as the socialization of things, where things communicate with other things – near and far. The power of locally connected things is a game changer for local economies, in both urban and rural communities. From the energy grid, to water supply systems, roads, trains, farms, schools, factories, hospitals, healthcare workers, and first responders the connectivity of things is becoming an enabler for economic prosperity. The emerging economy is shifting from a financial services economy to a cloud economy, from wall street to main street – the local economy, from smart cities and buildings in your neighborhood to smart factories and smart transportation in your state. We are in the midst of yet another technology revolution.

By most leading indicators globalization of trade is slowing down due to geopolitical events, labor unrest, and structural forces across the globe. What does this mean for globalization of data? Data is the fuel that powers a cloud economy. There are no tariffs on data (at least, not yet). Data will drive decisions, actions and outcomes at the local, state, regional, national and international stage, at times of growth or recession, peace or war. Technology is already driving this transformation. As past generations dealt with semiconductors, mainframes, personal computers, rotary dial phones, dial-up lines, to get to where we are today with hand- held devices, data centers and high-speed Internet, the next generation will witness the dawn of yet another wave – the digital clouds of change.

Just as wireless was the fastest and most efficient means to connect people across the globe in the 1990s, without audacious infrastructure projects to lay copper cables from the first mile to the last mile, the concept of edge cloud computing and storage are key factors in bringing digital transformation to the masses across the globe. This will give impetus to a new wave of global commerce, information sharing, and cybersecurity in a world without international firewalls. Even as a rotary dial phone transformed into a smart phone you carry in your pocket today and stay connected with the world, non-personal devices are becoming ubiquitous in the world around us in our homes, streets, cities and workplaces. As we transition from a "need to know" to "need to share" mindset on information exchange, data sharing – as trusted real-time feeds and as historical markers – will drive policies and processes of daily living from travel, events, social activities, news cycles, public utilities, and the job market.

The cloud is for the Internet of Things what software defined networking was for virtualized data centers. In fact, it is much more than just connectivity. The volume, variety and velocity of information from millions of devices will make it difficult to transport data to backend compute engines. Therefore, instead of pumping data to compute, compute must go to where the data is – at the edge. The data in this case will be a heterogenous set of information purposed for telemetry, measurements, facial recognition, crowd sensing, street surveillance, traffic congestion control, license plate recognition, financial services, soil monitoring, air quality monitoring, and plenty more. The potential is beyond imagination.

For innovators, technocrats and cybersecurity hawks, this means the promise and realization of 5G, edge computing, blockchain, post quantum cryptography, and containerization of applications and services. This will impact the next generation of consumer devices from entertainment set top boxes to home security monitoring systems, smart appliances, water management, air conditioning and heating systems. This will transform safety systems from building management to transportation and aviation systems. This will modernize national defense from battle equipment to soldier protection. The operations workflow from the manufacturing shop floor to field operations in the wild, and the maintenance of devices with a decade (or more) of lifespan will witness a gradual but imminent transformation, powered by service automation from a cloud of clouds. Instead of a centralized cloud, the Internet of Things will require a "trust chain of connected clouds".

Digital transformation is on trajectory to drive innovation in edge protection, process automation, and embedded mission-critical operations. Much of critical public infrastructure, utility grids, and industrial control systems are currently outdated and not cyber-protected. Imminent risks have no term limits. The emerging ecosystem of distributed computing will require a higher degree of trust in device identification, device authentication, permissioned admission controls and tamper-resistant content delivery. Further, this must be rooted in the notion of trustworthy ubiquitous devices and trusted data to power decision logic – namely process or policy-based actions. Untrusted devices and data without trust attribution will produce undesirable, and potentially tragic, outcomes. Therefore, it is time to collaborate at the grassroots level with the semiconductor industry, device vendors and service providers to make them trustworthy for induction into the lights-out automated ecosystem of connected clouds.

Chapter 8

The State of Digital Transformation and OT-IT Convergence

As we approach the end of an unforgettable year, all industries are recovering from the aftereffects of the global pandemic and contemplating the meaning and purpose of digital transformation. The goals of OT/IT (Operational Technology/Information Technology) convergence are far from cohesive, the associated investment costs remain constraining, and pathways to revenues appear fluid – for key stakeholders to commit to and execute on a roadmap. The collaborative nature of such an endeavor to transform legacy systems in critical infrastructure crammed with heterogeneous brownfield and greenfield devices is a daunting prospect. It will require equipment manufacturers, service providers, cloud platform vendors, and device owners/operators to agree on fundamental aspects of change (whose turf is this to lead the charge?).

The OT/IT Global Market Survey

To initiate an open dialog, we at Mocana conducted a global market survey to solicit views from key stakeholders and security professionals in the field of OT and IT. The survey respondents, who lead the charge in the battle to protect mission critical devices from cyber risks, provided us their perspectives and challenges as they embark on digital transformation in their respective industry segment. This whitepaper describes our findings and our proposed objectives to empower chief risk officers, solution architects, device vendors, owners and operators on this journey to design and build the next generation of smart connected things – for smart cities, smart homes, smart factories, smart buildings, smart transportation, and smart national defense (yes, we left nothing behind including the kitchen sink).

By all analyst projections, we see an emerging wave in OT/IT convergence that will drive adoption of digital transformation with standards and compliance-based objectives. OT/IT convergence for digital transformation requires a horizontal platform and collaborative effort for multi-tenant scalability (up and out), low latency, device interoperability, and subscription-based services. The opportunities for on-premise and cloud-based managed security service providers are immense, with a subscription-based utility model to manage cyber risks as IoT devices proliferate and penetrate all industry sectors. The OT/IT convergence wave will sweep across brownfield and greenfield devices offering a unified, streamlined, and non-disruptive workflow.

The OT/IT Global Market Survey Findings

Q1: Which of the following industry standards for cybersecurity are driving your focus in OT for digital transformation?

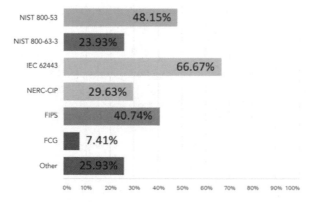

Figure 10: Survey Question #1

Q2: Which of the following risks in OT do you consider as imminent and worthy of attention?

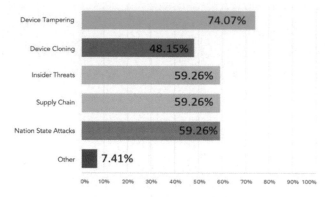

Figure 11: Survey Question #2

Q3: Which of the following capabilities do you believe device owners/operators would benefit the most from for OT/IT convergence and a unified workflow?

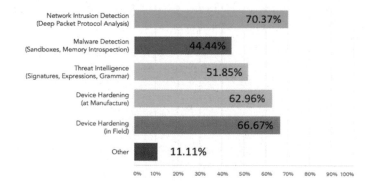

Figure 12: Survey Question #3

Q4: Which of the following mitigation actions do you believe would offer substantial cost savings to device owners/operators in OT after a cybersecurity-related incident?

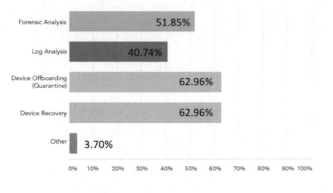

Figure 13: Survey Question #4

Q5: Which of the following countermeasures do you believe would make brownfield (legacy) devices most secure?

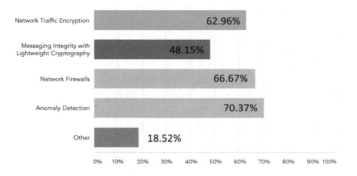

Figure 14: Survey Question #5

Q6: Which of the following countermeasures do you believe would make greenfield devices most secure?

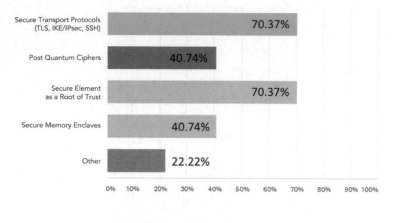
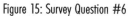

Figure 15: Survey Question #6

Q7: Which of the following controls do you believe would make OT devices most secure?

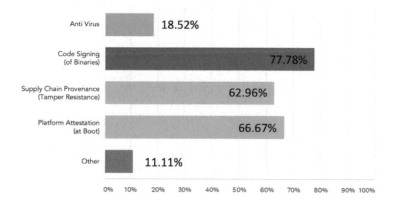
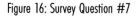

Figure 16: Survey Question #7

Q8: Which types of audits do you believe would make OT devices most compliant with cybersecurity standards?

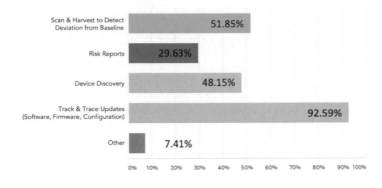

Figure 17: Survey Question #8

Q9: Which types of security controls do you believe makes inter-device communications most trustworthy?

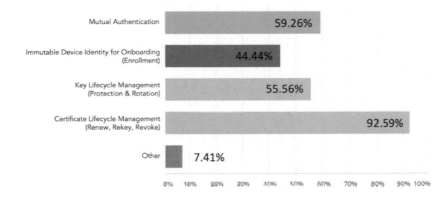

Figure 18: Survey Question #9

Q10: Which types of OT devices do you believe require protection controls?

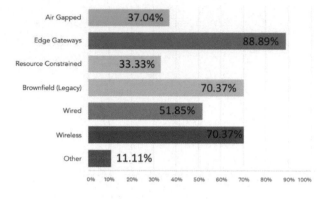

Figure 19: Survey Question #10

Q11: Which of the following restrictions do you believe are consequential for device vendors in the fragmented global market of IIoT/IoT?

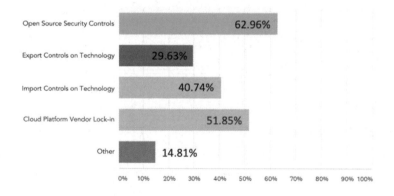

Figure 20: Survey Question #11

Q12: What would be the most effective long-term strategy for device vendors for productization and secure interoperability with emerging technologies?

Figure 21: Survey Question #12

Q13: Which of the following forms of communications are applicable to your industry sector?

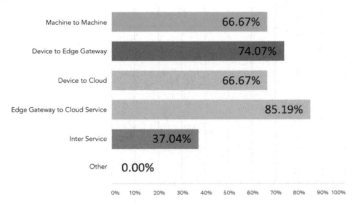

Figure 22: Survey Question #13

Q14: Which of the following platforms are applicable to your industry?

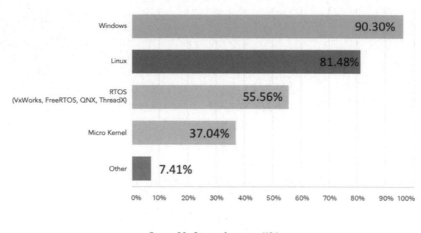

Figure 23: Survey Question #14

Q15: Which of the following regions are applicable to your market?

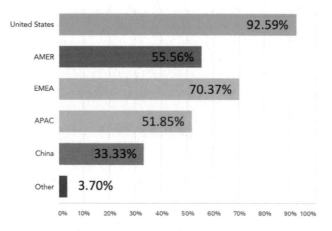

Figure 24: Survey Question #15

The Key Factors for Stakeholders

The survey responses provided us their insights into key factors that are broadly influencing stakeholders and decision makers about the evolutionary trajectory of devices in narrow-band and broad-band IoT domains.

- Device Tampering
- Device Cloning
- Device Hardening
- Zero Trust Infrastructure with Mutual Authentication and Secure Elements
- Device Recovery
- Track and Trace Updates
- Supply Chain Provenance
- Network Traffic Encryption with Pathway to Post Quantum Cryptography
- Standards & Compliance
- Network Segmentation

Goals for OT/IT Convergence

To paraphrase the proposed goals in one mission statement: "OT/IT convergence for digital transformation requires developing seven habits of trustworthy devices, five degrees of device protection, and three rings of resilience in cyber space". The reincarnation of devices must begin with the "transformation" objective. There can be no digital transformation without the transformation predicate.

Chapter 9

The Building Blocks for Device Transformation

The Seven Habits of Trustworthy Devices

Old habits die hard, bad habits die harder (factory default passwords, unprotected passwords on autonomous devices, implicit/assumed trust, plain text communications, dearth of forensic logs, theft of unprotected intellectual property and mission data at rest). Device transformation is an essential component of digital transformation. The habits to achieve trustworthiness must span over the device life cycle from the time of manufacture, through the lifetime of provisioning, operations, and maintenance in the field, to decommissioning (revocation/removal) of cryptographic artifacts on the device.

Figure 25: The Seven Habits of Trustworthy Devices

The Five Degrees of Device Protection

The level of protection that a particular device warrants will vary based on device function, resource constraints, cost of harm on compromise, and the price of hardening (at manufacture or in-field retrofit) amortized over the lifetime of the device in the field. The five degrees of device protection are: device identification, device authentication, key protection, data protection and operational trustworthiness. The security controls required depend on the capabilities of the underlying hardware platform and the desired level of cybersecurity compliance based on the industry segment.

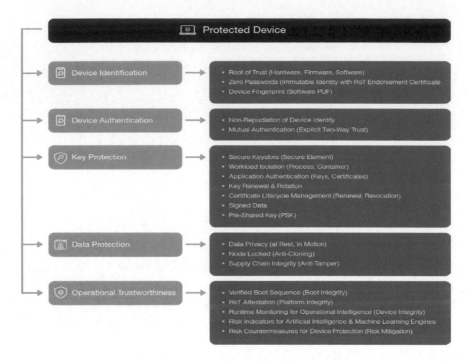

Figure 26: The Five Degrees of Protection

The Three Rings of Resilience

Building perpetual resilience requires a foundation of trust at the core, a shield of protective countermeasures against insider and external threats, and measurement-based risk indicators for AI/ML powered timely and remote intervention. The pathways to cost effective distributed risk management, operational efficiencies, and subscription-based services rooted in a public/ private/community cloud-based platform would be illuminated by these rings of resilience.

Figure 27: The Three Rings of Resilience

OT/IT convergence for digital transformation requires a horizontal platform and collaborative effort for device vendors and end users to realize the benefits and efficiencies of smart connected things. It will require investment in innovation and modernization from silicon transformation (e.g. integrated/embedded SIMs, TPMs, Intel® EPID) to shifting clouds (5G & Multi-Access Edge Computing, containerized applications) with a clear line of sight grounded in device reincarnation. From corporate board of directors, CISOs and chief risk officers, to solution architects, program/product managers, and developers, the road to an integrated OT/IT architecture with a unified workflow will require weighing the cost of status quo versus the price of modernization leveraging emerging technologies – such as secure elements, edge compute, and wireless/5G networking – for multi-tenant scalability (up and out), low latency, device interoperability, and subscription-based services.

Chapter 10

When the Supply Chain Becomes the Kill Chain

Tragically, the hackers have won yet again defeating security profession-als, processes, and technology. The recent wave of successful cybersecu-rity attacks on key United States agencies, large organizations, and security companies underscores the fundamental inadequacies of the detection and forensic analysis (post breach) based tool chest that is pervasive in the infor-mation technology (IT) industry today. Hackers possess an arsenal of toolkits to discover and infect monitored systems with published exposures. Threat hunting and trusted intelligence, while essential, are insufficient as these attacks have proven once again. The threat hunter is also the hunted in this infinite war of will and resources. Once again, the low and slow attacks evaded and outpaced discovery and timely incident response. The security operations center (SOC) needs a changeup.

The cybersecurity disposition is at crossroads, again. The millions of sys-tems and billions of devices that are at risk of cyber-attack are not only fragile but proliferating in our daily lives, at work, in public, and at home. Unless these systems and devices are designed for resilience and tamper resistance, there is no protection on the road ahead. Protection is an attribute of deep-rooted design; detection is an afterthought. The root cause lies in the limitations of the means and methods. The battlefield of cybersecurity is vast and lies outside the enterprise information technology (IT) perimeter. Systems are vulnerable because they are purpose built to perform specific collaborative functions, not self-defense. This is the "soft core, hard edge" ecosystem that poses the herculean "finding the needle in the growing haystack" challenge to SOC operators.

The fundamental paradigm shift that is required to reverse the alarming trend is to differentiate threats from risks. Chasing threats (hunters) does not mitigate long term supply chain risks (farmers). There is no truth in data, just probabilities. Relying on threat intelligence as the sole source of decision logic is a deficient analytics engine (false positives, true negatives). To defuse landed threats, risks have to be anticipated and protective countermeasures baked in. The greatest risks today are in the blind spots created by an implicit trust in the supply chain, content updates to field systems and devices (firmware, software, configuration, operational datasets), and the global staging surface for orchestrated attacks by nation state actors. The weaknesses in authentication methods and zero-touch ceremonies, while convenient for users, poses grave risks (pandora's box) without immutable identities, digital certificates, and a root of trust. The digitally transformed ecosystem that is becoming autonomous and brokerless introduces blind spots for traditional methods of activity monitoring and compliance audits in the absence of platform hardening.

From public safety systems to public utilities, industrial control systems, and consumer electronics, the target for attackers is a greenfield opportunity. The lack of resolve amongst political committees, bureaucrats, and regulators has emboldened the cybercrime syndicate. The alarming trend in the transition from user psychology grade email phishing attacks, watering hole attacks, social networking exploits, to enterprise grade ransomware and supply chain attacks is a compelling indicator of device vendors, equipment manufacturers, and software vendors letting the guard down against a determined and tenacious adversary. Unless embedded protection becomes a mandatory attribute to qualify devices as trustworthy, the supply chain is at imminent risk of becoming the kill chain in the years ahead.

On the uphill road to OT/IT convergence, CISOs, risk officers and cyber insurers must judiciously evaluate innovative technologies and avoid the pitfalls of relying exclusively on incumbent network grammar and anomaly-based detection technologies. A cyberattack on operational technology (OT) will have staggering consequences from service outages to in-field manual intervention, and large-scale device recalls. The stakes are astoundingly high and therefore device protection for long term device lifecycle management is critical. Cyber-attacks on OT devices prevail because of the risks device owners and operators are willing to take. Embarking on digital transformation without asset protection for cyber resilience will lead to IoT paralysis and brand damage down the road.

"When the Gods wish to punish us, they answer our prayers"

— Oscar Wilde

Chapter 11

The Conundrums of Trust

Convergence of Information Technology (IT) and Operational Technology (OT) to secure the Internet of Things (IoT), the Industrial IoT (IIoT), and OT solutions will eventually follow the route towards continuous surveillance that the IT world navigated over the past two decades. The imminent risks with connected devices today are not an IT, IoT, or OT specific problem to categorize as. The fundamental cracks are the grade of technology and level of protection embedded in these devices before they are deployed in the field and provisioned for operation by conventional device management systems. Operational Risk (OR) management requires attention to device security by design, and not just device function by purpose.

The IT Conundrum

Pin-holing the perimeter defenses (demilitarized zone) exposed the air gapped and segmented Enterprise networks – to external users for remote access, and to internal users for cloud hosted services. This confluence of public and private ecosystems led to a cascade effect of security controls from network traffic inspection for intrusion detection and prevention (the network operations center or NOC), to security information and event monitoring systems (the security operations center or SOC), platform hardening checklists, vulnerability assessment standards (NIST SCAP/CVEs, STIG, STIX/TAXII, et al), and ultimately endpoint-based countermeasures for detection and prevention of landed malware and resident exploits. The operative phrase for IT SOC was "threat intelligence".

The Cloud Conundrum

IT outsourcing, data center virtualization, and cloud bursting led to "securing the cloud" (with cloud access security brokers, multi-factor authentication) and "security in the cloud" (with full stack hardening, process isolation, secure enclaves, cryptographic encryption of data lakes). With the migration of applications and data to public, private and community clouds, privacy and confidentiality concerns emerged. The software-as-a-service (SaaS) model shifted the onus of security to SaaS vendors as the guardians of multi-tenancy. The cloud became the home away from home for users and applications. The operative phrase for cloud SOC was "visibility and control in the fog".

The OT Conundrum

The emerging wave of digital transformation across industry sectors from industrial control systems, to healthcare, manufacturing, transportation, public utilities, critical infrastructure and defense requires a paradigm shift. Unlike Enterprise IT endpoints (user workstations, server farms, and network elements), the needs of OT are radically different. OT requires runtime operational integrity monitoring, field device hardening (of brownfield and greenfield devices), and supply chain risk management. These are not standalone solutions. They require a holistic and interconnected suite of specialized risk controls and countermeasures. The cloud is now homing in on devices. The operative phrase for OT SOC is "risk intelligence".

The Digital Transformation Conundrum

IT-OT convergence will require traditional IT SOC teams to operate outside their comfort zone with OT field operators. Digital Transformation requires collaboration between silicon chip vendors, original device vendors, certificate authorities, managed security service providers, and cloud platform vendors. Digital Transformation is fundamentally about life cycle management of a diverse set of devices (from Linux/Windows/Mac OS platforms to

VxWorks/FreeRTOS/QNX RTOS platforms, tablets, and smartphones) from the manufacturing line to field deployment, device health monitoring, and condition-based maintenance. The frictionless surface for artificial intelligence (AI) and machine learning (ML) in OT applications begins with an intelligent device designed for tamper resistance, trusted content delivery, attested metrics, and remote recovery. The vast investments in digital transformation and 5G require value creation from embedded trust in devices to a low latency services platform at edge gateways for OT economics at scale and ROI. While CISOs and CIOs implement a strategic plan with security controls to optimize workflow and manage threats, CTOs and product security architects must design with protection controls to transform devices and manage risks. Security is a control; but Trust is a chain.

Chapter 12

The Risk Model

In sharp contrast to the threat intelligence-based IT detection and prevention strategy, IoT and OT device protection requires a risk intelligence-based mindset. The onus of tamper evidence and operational resilience required for risk management is distributed across the supply chain.

Device Vendor Scenario	Risks & Exposures	Security Countermeasures	Compliance Violation	Security Breach	Safety Risk
Cloned Device	Loss of Revenue	Immutable ID of Secure Element, Certificate Revocation			●
Manual Device Registration (Factory)	Cumbersome Inventory Configuration Management	Tamper Resistant Manufacturing Workflow	●		
Manual Device Onboarding (In-Field)	Cumbersome Provisioning and Asset Tracking	Secure Device Authentication and Transfer of Ownership			●
Factory Key Compromise	Device Recall with Fused Silicon Vendor or OEM Key	Remote Key Management/Renewal		●	
Compromise of Device Credentials	Default/Weak Password Breach	Key/Certificate Based Authentication		●	
Operation Tampering	Loss of Trust in Device Function	Boot and Runtime Trust Metrics	●		●
Data Tampering	Loss of Message Integrity, Data Based Attacks	Sign and Verify with Protected Keys	●	●	●
Data Privacy	Theft of User Information or Data	Seal and/or Encrypt to a Local Secure Element	●		
Subverted (Compromised) Device	Open Surface for DDoS Attacks, Service Outage	Supply Chain Provenance of Executable & Configuration Bitstreams	●	●	●
Key Lifecycle Management	Single Key Compromise Bricks Device	Automate Key Renewal with Algorithmic Agility		●	
Bricked Device Recovery	Long Duration Service Disruption	Remote Updates (to Factory Default)	●		
Unauthorized Remote Access	Device Configuration Tampering, Loss of Intellectual Property	Embedded Perimeter Controls	●	●	
Isolation of Containerized Applications	Co-resident Attacker, Side Channel (Lateral) Attacks	Virtualization of Trust Anchor	●	●	
Boot Integrity (Platform)	Root Kit, Boot Kit, Insecure Key Store	Multi-Stage, Multi-Key Verification	●	●	●
Tamper Resistant Updates (Platform)	Lack of Trust in Supply Chain Integrity	Multiple Signatories for Multi-Factor Verification	●	●	●

Figure 28: The Risk Model

Device Protection

Digital transformation of traditional original equipment manufacturer (OEM) product and solution offerings requires hardening of connected and edge devices with a horizontal platform that provides a single pane of glass for operations technology (OT) security. Deploying greenfield devices in traditional network silos alongside legacy brownfield devices in OT environments introduces major risks and exposes a huge attack surface for cyber warfare. The imminent threats, posed by the cybercrime syndicate and nation state actors targeting critical infrastructure and unprotected devices, warrant establishing a trust chain for supply chain risk management as a collaborative effort between OEMs, brand name device vendors, and managed security service providers (MSSPs).

The primary goal of digital transformation should be to manufacture devices at scale for supply chain risk management and operational resilience with visibility and control for tamper-resistance, anti-cloning, and condition-based monitoring/maintenance (CBM). The transformation must begin at the device. The passage to digital transformation requires all stakeholders to recognize the following realisms:

- IIoT/IoT is an ecosystem that requires a horizontal platform.
- A collaborative effort is required between OEMs, brand name device vendors, and MSSPs for cost-effective cyber protection as a service.
- OT/IT convergence requires a paradigm shift.
- Integration of emerging and emerged technologies for an epical (Economical, Political, Intellectual, Commercial) story.

With this as the context for digital transformation, the seven habits of highly trustworthy devices may be enumerated as follows.

1) Persistence of Trust

- Establish and preserve device trustworthiness throughout the lifecycle.

- Ensure that data harvested and processed for analytics by artificial intelligence (AI) and machine learning (ML) engines is trustworthy for safe and secure mission critical decision logic and outcomes.

2) Reduces Lifetime Costs

- Reduce the OEM's and Enterprise's capital and operational expenses.

- Scale and automate manufacturing, deployment, and lifetime monitoring of heterogeneous connected and edge devices.

3) Manages Supply Chain Risks

- Manage supply chain risks with tamper-resistant content delivery.

- Track and trace along the supply chain from the developer, though providers and publishers to the target OT device.

4) Recovers to a Trusted State

- Remotely orchestrate field device recovery and mitigate service outages.

- Remotely rollback images and/or configurations to a trusted baseline.

- Remotely rotate cryptographic artifacts (keys, certificates) to minimize exposure to potential exploits.

5) Protects Data in Custody

- Protect data (at-rest, in-process, in-transit) in the custody of mission critical native and/or containerized applications.

- Use a secure element as the hardware, firmware, or software-based root of trust.

6) Protects Digital Assets

- Prevent theft of intellectual property and/or mission critical data by untrusted devices.

- Prevent cloning of trusted devices.

7) Achieves Compliance

- Provide security controls required for compliance with emerging standards and certifications for cybersecurity and multi-vendor field device interoperability.

- IEC 62443/61850, NIST 800-53/800-63-3, NERC CIP, FIPS 140-2/140-3, FCG, IEEE 802.1AR.

Device protection is based on five pillars of risk: device identification, device authentication, key protection, data protection and operational trustworthiness. The security, safety, and economics of designing and implementing risk countermeasures in trustworthy devices will far outweigh the cost of innovation for key players in the IoT ecosystem.

In the rapidly emerging IoT industry segments, such as smart buildings, smart factories, smart cities and smart energy, there are revenue drivers and return on investment (ROI) associated with transforming device management with applied data sciences and subscription-based cloud services. Within the next two years, emerging 5G and secure element (e.g. TPM, SIM) enabled services will lead to a proliferation of heterogeneous connected and edge devices in traditional Enterprise managed ecosystems, and present new challenges in OT/IT convergence and integration with cloud platform providers without vendor lock-in.

Chapter 13

The Uphill Road to OT-IT Convergence

Across all the major industry sectors, chief risk officers, product managers, solution architects and subject matter experts have to confront the economic, political, intellectual and commercial challenges of industrial and non-industrial IoT with a subjective assessment of the following fundamental introspections.

The Road

1) As the end user of IoT devices, where do I start with digital transformation of brownfield and greenfield devices?

   Begin with hardening of greenfield devices, in-field or at the point of manufacture, for coexistence with brownfield devices. Then proceed with hardening of RTOS based brownfield devices through a device vendor-initiated update cycle.

2) As a CISO, how should I budget for device hardening and risk management? What are the capital and operational expenses that I should plan for?

   Device hardening requires planning to coordinate updates through the device vendors and line of business (LOB) application developers as part of an update cycle. A risk management service requires a hosting platform, on-premise or in the cloud. The operational aspects of the risk management service must provide long-term cost reduction with remote orchestration and SoC for security, monitoring, and recovery.

3) Should I manage the transformation program beginning at the device level though OEMs, or directly through device vendors, or at the services level through managed security service providers?

This may require a multi-phase approach depending on your target environment and compliance requirements. The quick start zero-coding first phase may be to work with equipment and device manufacturers to instrument the device platforms. The next step may be to work with a managed security service provider (MSSP) for subscription-based services for instrumented devices. The final step may be to coordinate with device vendors and application developers for ubiquity across device platforms for a unified approach, and a single pane of glass.

4) Which industry standards for cybersecurity are driving my focus in OT for digital transformation?

- NIST 800-53
- NIST 800-63-3
- IEEE 802.1AR
- IEC 62443
- ISA 84
- NERC-CIP
- FIPS
- FCG
- ISO 27001

5) Which risks in OT do I consider as imminent and worthy of attention?

- Device Tampering

- Device Cloning
- Insider Threats
- Supply Chain
- Nation State Attacks
- Ransomware

6) Which capabilities do I believe device owners/operators would benefit the most from for OT/IT convergence and a unified workflow?

- Network Intrusion Detection (Deep Packet Protocol Analysis)
- Malware Detection (Sandboxes, Memory Introspection)
- Threat Intelligence (Signatures, Expressions, Grammar)
- Device Hardening (at Manufacture)
- Device Hardening (in Field)
- Zero Trust Infrastructure

7) Which mitigation actions do I believe would offer substantial cost savings to device owners/operators in OT after a cybersecurity related incident?

- Forensic Analysis
- Log Analysis
- Device Offboarding (Quarantine)
- Device Recovery

8) Which countermeasures do I believe would make brownfield (legacy) devices most secure?

- Network Traffic Encryption
- Messaging Integrity with Lightweight Cryptography
- Network Firewalls
- Anomaly Detection
- Allow Lists
- Network Segmentation

9) Which countermeasures do I believe would make greenfield devices most secure?

- Secure Transport Protocols (TLS, IKE/IPsec, SSH)
- Post Quantum Ciphers
- Secure Element as a Root of Trust
- Secure Memory Enclaves
- Mutual Authentication
- Zero Trust (Fingerprints, Certificates)

10) Which controls do I believe would make OT devices most secure?

- Anti-Virus
- Code Signing (of Binaries)
- Supply Chain Provenance (Tamper Resistance)
- Platform Attestation (at Boot)
- Mutual Authentication

11) Which types of audits do I believe would make OT devices most compliant with cybersecurity standards?

- Scan & Harvest to Detect Deviation from Baseline
- Risk Reports
- Device Discovery
- Track & Trace Updates (Software, Firmware, Configuration)

12) Which types of security controls do I believe makes inter-device communications most trustworthy?

- Mutual Authentication
- Immutable Device Identity for Onboarding (Enrollment)
- Key Lifecycle Management (Protection & Rotation)
- Certificate Lifecycle Management (Renew, Rekey, Revoke)
- Post Quantum Cryptography

13) Which types of OT devices do I believe require protection controls?

- Air Gapped

- Edge Gateways

- Resource Constrained

- Brownfield (Legacy)

- Wired

- Wireless

14) Which restrictions do I believe are consequential for device vendors in the fragmented global market of IIoT/IoT?

- Open-Source Security Controls

- Export Controls on Technology

- Import Controls on Technology

- Cloud Platform Vendor Lock-in

15) What would be the most effective long-term strategy for device vendors for productization and secure interoperability with emerging technologies?

- Open-Source Security Components

- Build a Proprietary Solution

- Build a Standards Based Solution

- Buy a Standards Based Commercial Solution

The Climb

In the end, the primary use cases and industry specific needs will drive the desired solution. The overarching objective of digital transformation however must be to connect OT devices in cyberspace with embedded safety and protection countermeasures for scalability, visibility, control, and a single pane of glass for field operators. This will necessitate a horizontal platform with core capabilities and intrinsic functions to address:

- Device Tampering

- Device Cloning

- Device Hardening
- Zero Trust Infrastructure with Mutual Authentication and Secure Elements
- Device Recovery
- Track and Trace Updates
- Supply Chain Provenance
- Network Traffic Encryption with Pathway to Post Quantum Cryptography
- Standards & Compliance (e.g. NIST, IEC, NERC-CIP)
- Network Segmentation

The Escalator

A solution architecture based on the operations, analytics and development platforms provides a framework for the seven habits of trustworthy devices, the five degrees of protection, and the three rings of resilience required for OT/IT convergence.

"The only constant is change, continuing change, inevitable change, that is the dominant factor in society today. No sensible decision can be made any longer without taking into account not only the world as it is, but the world as it will be"

— Isaac Asimov

Chapter 14

Why Breaches Happen

B reaches happen not because of a single point of failure but because of a series of failures. The root cause is the evidence analysis gap – real-time behavior and context introspection. Automation increases the velocity of decision – by augmenting human decisions with expert systems. Diversity of analytics models is essential to strategically minimize residual risks.

No intricate grid of security point controls howsoever strategically deployed at the perimeter and in the core of the network can respond reliably and effectively without real-time threat information sharing. Actionable intelligence will require risk metrics, interoperability across multi-vendor security products, velocity of remediation (facilitated by REST APIs without a human-in-the-loop) and diversity of detection methods for resilience against advanced evasion techniques of emerging threats. There is no locality of reference and the symptoms may occur far from the root cause - a ripple effect. Information fusion from a combination of complementary solutions is required to establish context, reduce uncertainty and minimize "known unknowns". Velocity of decision requires automated analytics as a component of the decision logic.

The users' view of Cyber is a "world wide web". The security practitioners view of Cyber is "who, what, why". Network access is a privilege which may be abused to infiltrate malware or exfiltrate data that may be harmful to the enterprise. Relying on signatures and "known knowns" is ineffective against targeted threats and sandboxing technologies are vulnerable to obfuscation. Neither a bump-in-the-wire nor a bump-in-the-stack model is scalable for continuous runtime integrity monitoring for lateral movement and across the perimeter.

The key drivers for action by a review board are the perceived reality of the threat, impact realization to justify the need for timely response, and compelling evidence that the enterprise is a target. The key indicators of risk, the traditional checklist approach and enterprise risk management (Measure Your Risk) may be described as follows:

Indicator	Monitored Object	Checklist Paradigm	Traditional Approach	Residual Risks (Challenges)	Measure Your Risk
Who	User	Identity Management	Strict Password Policy, Multi-Factor Authentication	Impersonation, Delegation, Compromised Credentials, Flow Integrity	Behaviors (Remote Access, Partners, Supply Chain, Anonymous)
What	Application	File Reputation	Allow & Deny Lists	Runtime Operational Integrity	Evidence (Callbacks, Obfuscation, Anti-Detection Techniques)
Why	Action	Compliance & Audit Program	Role Based Access Controls, Static & Dynamic Separation of Duties	Cross Domain, Cross Border, Multi Tenancy	Context (Signaling Integrity, Data Exchange)

In today's enterprise IT environment, users and devices far outnumber administrators. The user is the weak link and therefore automation is key for continuous vigilance. The division of roles and responsibilities between network, system, database, application and domain administrators is likely to introduce blind spots that malware and cyber criminals can exploit through social engineering and process gap exploits.

Over the past three decades, the ecosystem has evolved from centralized mainframe computing (heavy metal, tightly coupled systems) with dumb terminals and keyboards, to distributed client-server computing with workstations over TCP/IP, to virtualization with hypervisors (bare metal fluid platforms) and cloud services (vapor ware, loosely coupled) where the web browser is the ubiquitous client and the product is a service orchestrated as a three-tier stack (web, application and database silos). Detection methodologies must therefore evolve to encompass the paradigm shift as these intricacies warrant a behavior-based approach to measure runtime operational integrity of the infrastructure, platform and services layers for post-infection pre-breach markers. The staging surface is wide and inadequately instrumented without the "who, what, why" visibility.

A redundant security stack and automated analytics are essential to build fault tolerance in the decision logic to reduce false negatives for timely analysis of post-infection pre-breach evidence.

The Economic Loss

1) Breach Analysis
   - Forensic Investigations
   - Fines and Penalties

2) Black Market Value
   - Stolen Intellectual Property
   - Stolen Client Information

3) Damaged Asset Recovery
   - Data Hijack or Erasure
   - Internet of Things (Production Equipment, Critical Infrastructure & Devices)

4) Business Continuity
   - Toxic Inventory Scrubbing
   - Data Cleansing

5) Service Outages
   - The cost of harm in IoT and OT ecosystems includes disruption of essential services (e.g. electric grids, water treatment plants, manufacturing systems, transportation systems) as an instrument of cyberwar by nation state actors.

6) Public Safety Hazard
   - The tragic loss of human lives that may be caused by service outages triggered by cyber-attacks on public utilities and safety systems may reach staggering levels (comparable to natural disasters).

Chapter 15

Signaling Integrity and Data Exchanges

Traditional security technologies including detection and defense technologies such as legacy and currently available anti-virus software, network firewalls, and intrusion detection/prevention systems depend on signatures to monitor threats and attacks. Increasingly sophisticated emerging threats and attacks are developing techniques for evading these traditional detection and defense technologies. For example, a threat may modify its signature in an attempt to remain undetected by traditional technologies. Other threats may detect the presence of traditional detection and defense techniques and employ methods tailored to avoid detection.

Traditional detection and defense techniques tend to be based on a hard-edge and soft-core architecture. Some examples of techniques employed at the hard edge are security appliances such as network firewalls and intrusion detection/prevention systems. Examples of techniques employed at the soft core are antivirus and network-based integrity measurement and verification services that scan and audit business critical systems, services, and high value data silos. When the hard edge is breached, however, these defensive methods are largely ineffective in: (a) protecting vulnerable or compromised systems, (b) providing any level of assurance of the runtime operational integrity of the soft core, (c) preventing exfiltration of information from compromised systems, and (d) blocking exfiltration of information due to rogue insiders within the enterprise.

Typically, advanced threats have a life cycle where the threat is delivered, where the threat evades detection, and where the threat persists and takes hold. During each of these stages, signals to and from internal and external actors are transmitted and received from the portion of the advanced threat that has been delivered into an enterprise. Although enterprises are aware of at least some of these threats, the traditional defense and detection techniques that are employed tend to use pattern matching or other signature matching algorithms to detect intrusions. Other traditional techniques employ reputation-based lists of network addresses or domains in an effort to detect threats.

The authors of malware and other threats are aware of traditional defense and detection techniques and have adapted their threats to evade and avoid such defenses. For example, advanced threats may use multiple networks to extract information from an enterprise or use seemingly benign data flows to camouflage the extraction of information. Other advanced threats may detect attempts to detect and decipher activity by detecting the presence of sandboxing or virtual machine execution. In response, these advanced threats may use delayed or conditional unpacking of code, content obfuscation, adaptive signaling, dynamic domains, IP and domain fluxing, and other techniques to evade traditional detection and defense techniques.

One example is when advanced threats leverage the syntax of standards-based protocols, like Hypertext Transmission Protocol (HTTP), to transmit information. Traditional defense and detection techniques do not examine the information exchanged over these standards-based protocols because any violations in the protocol are addressed by the application, not the transport or networking infrastructure. This allows advanced threats to use standards-based channels to transmit signals for command-and-control purposes and information extracted from data silos without being detected through conventional techniques. Other times, advanced threats will conform to the appropriate standard, but will employ encoded, encrypted, or otherwise obfuscated malicious communications in an effort to evade detection. In still other situations, advanced threats will conform to applicable standards and indicate that the transported content is of one type, but in fact transport content of another type. For example, the advanced threat may declare that the information being transferred is an image file when the information is in fact an executable binary. Therefore, a need for a solution that offers a way to reliably examine the signaling integrity and data exchanges of an application or service operating on a computing device.

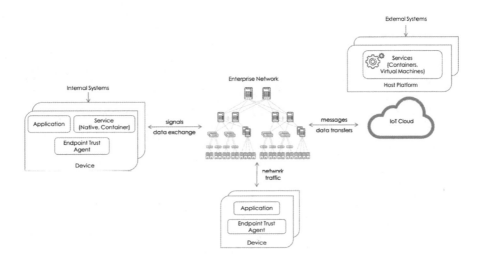

Figure 29: Signaling & Data Exchange

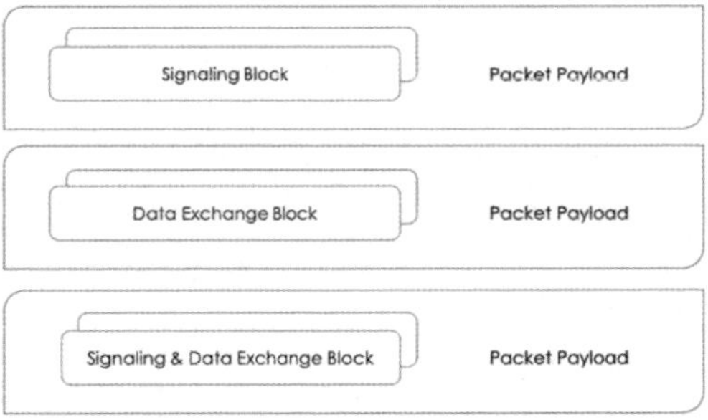

Figure 30: Identifying Signaling & Data Exchange Blocks

Chapter 16

Runtime Operational Integrity

Threat Identification

The method provides passive observations-based intelligence correlation and network application monitoring. The method provides runtime operational integrity of a system by receiving a dynamic context including endpoint events and network endpoint assessments. The method also generates temporal events based on the network endpoint assessments and correlates the endpoint events and temporal events before generating an integrity profile for the system. In another embodiment, flow level remediation is provided to isolate infected or compromised systems from a computing network fabric using a network trust agent, an endpoint trust agent, and a trust orchestrator.

Subject Reputation Score

The method provides reputation scores for network services and transactions to determine security risks. The security risks are calculated by determining subject reputation scores. In an embodiment, a system receives a query for a reputation score of a subject, initiates directed queries to external information management systems to interrogate attributes associated with the subject and analyzes responses. The system receives a hierarchical subject reputation score based on a calculus of risk and returns a reputation token. In another embodiment, a method provides real time attestation of a subject's reputation to a service provider using an endpoint trust agent, and a trust orchestrator comprising a reputation broker and a trust broker.

Tiered Remediation

The method provides network flow and device level remediation in response to reconnaissance-based intelligence correlation based on network monitoring, to accomplish network flow remediation and device/platform remediation. In an embodiment, a system receives system warnings and endpoint threat intelligence. The system correlates risk based on inputs from sensory inputs that monitor network activity, system configuration, resource utilization, and device integrity. The system then performs a calculus of risk on a global security context including endpoint assessment reports and sends system warnings based upon the endpoint threat intelligence. The system includes a remediation engine for receiving real time directives to control the device.

Mobile Device Attestation

The method provides dynamic attestation of mobile device integrity based upon subject reputation scores. In an embodiment, the method scores trustworthiness of a mobile device based on reputation scores for users associated with the device and/or a device reputation score. The method generates runtime integrity alerts regarding execution anomalies for applications executing on the device, calculates risks based on a ruleset, and determines a calculus of risk for the device. The method sends endpoint events comprising data and content of the integrity warnings to a trust orchestrator, which generates an integrity profile based on the endpoint events.

Chapter 17

The Status Quo

Over the past decades, security has evolved as an afterthought from network edge (external) to device (internal) security controls that stacked up to build a multi-layer defense in depth strategy.

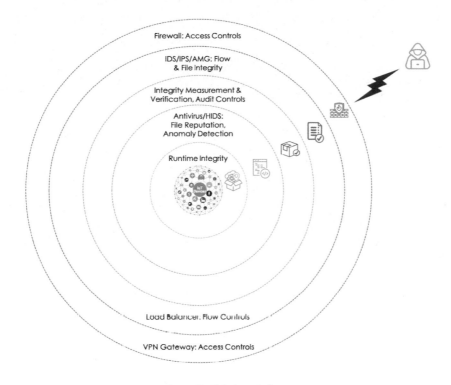

Figure 31: Multi-Layer Defense

The Cyber Turf

The moats and walls were designed to thwart a frontal attack by a traditional enemy in an open battlefield. As battles transformed into opaque cyber wars and insider threats staged by state actors, professional cyber-crime syndicates and hacktivists, the defenses proved ineffective and outdated for stealth and urban warfare. The enemy inside and out of sight poses a clear and present danger.

Hierarchical Enterprise Networks

Historically, the topology of enterprise networks has been hierarchical, from the demilitarized zone (DMZ) to the user silos and internal server farms (application, service, data silos), with zones established by virtual

LAN identifiers (VLAN) or subnets, and access control lists (ACLs) in a wiring closet of access, distribution and core switches and routers. Security was enforced by a set of authentication and authorization controls at the network and application layer to manage client-server and peer-to-peer computing and networking.

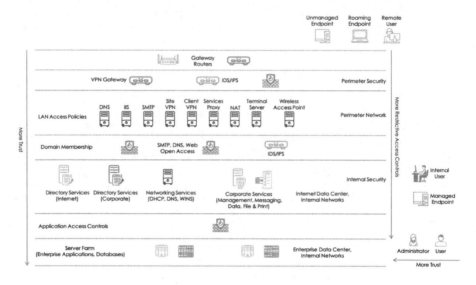

Figure 32: Tiered Network Topology

Stack Evolution

The evolution triggered by virtualization, software defined networking, and cloud-based utility models transformed the stack, and exemplified the difference between a risk and a threat, between implied and measured trust.

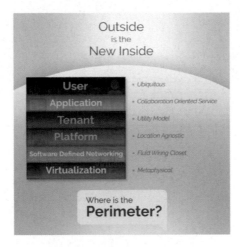

Figure 33: Stack Transformation

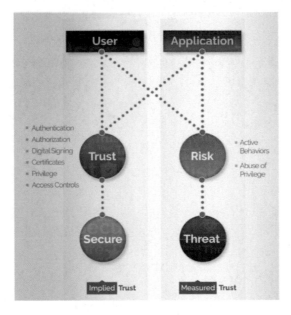

Figure 34: Levels of Trust

Access Management versus Entropy Management

The evolution from access management to entropy management was triggered by security considerations. Access management requires policy-driven permission controls based on object and action identifiers. Entropy management requires event-driven remediation controls based on threat or risk identifiers.

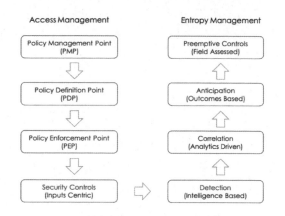

Figure 35: The Entropy Challenge

Attack in Depth

The bull's eye for the cybercrime syndicate is the soft core, not the hard edge. The hackers know how to deliver the malware (as web links, email attachments, audio/video/image files), evade the perimeter (signatures, pattern matching expressions, sandboxes), persist on a system (elude anti-virus file digests, heuristics), and take hold of the network (perform low and slow lateral reconnaissance to map out the landscape, decoys to subvert timely attention). Once inside the hard edge, it is a greenfield of opportunities for undetected malware.

Cybersecurity Gap Analysis

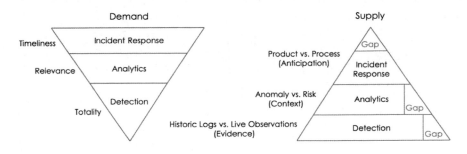

Figure 36: Innovation is in the Gap

Residual Risk

Threats to critical assets are generally addressed through well planned security controls driven by business needs, policies and instituted processes as the strategic layer of defense. Trust in these security controls is based on an input centric reliance on how they function. The difference between trustworthy and trusted actions produces residual risk.

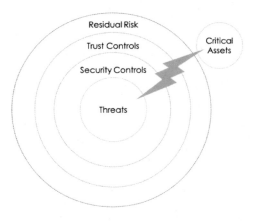

Figure 37: The Deficit of Trust

Dependency Chain

Any active risk management system requires timely evidence for preemptive Incident Response (IR) and rapid remediation. IR requires cross domain analytics for relevance of evidence. Analytics requires fine grained detection for totality of evidence.

Realms of Awareness

- Attribution aware (by subject: user, file, application, process, thread)
- Action aware (by function: activity, operation)
- Capability aware (by operation: hardware enhanced, atomic principle of least privilege)

Questionable Intelligence versus Actionable Intelligence

- Questionable intelligence suggests inadequate totality of indicators with contextual relevance for timely remediation
- Actionable intelligence requires evidence beyond reasonable doubt

Evidentiary Outcome versus Desired Outcome

- Evidentiary outcome stipulates that investigations begin without any hypothesis bias (innocent until proven guilty)
- Desired outcome infers investigation begins with a hypothesis bias (guilty until proven innocent).

Non-Hierarchical versus Hierarchical Trust

- Hierarchical Trust: Trusted (secure) data processed on a trusted (secure) platform by a trusted application. The vertical trust vector.
- Non-Hierarchical Trust: Integrity of data and operations in a cross realm (distributed) tightly or loosely coupled ecosystem (implicit trust). The horizontal trust vector.

Trusted Data

- Data at rest (protected by: static encryption, symmetric keys)
- Data in flight (protected by: dynamic encryption, asymmetric keys)
- Data in process (protected by: trusted container, capability-aware platform)

Trusted Execution versus Verifiable Trust

- Trusted execution is a form of implied trust.
- Verifiable trust is a means to establish a quantitative and qualitative measure of explicit trust.

The False Positive

False positives pose the biggest challenge and paranoia to security analysts. While false negatives are a clear failure to detect and/or analyze a security event, false positives receive time consuming examination prior to write-off. Nevertheless, suppressing a false positive due to lack of context may be a fallacy as a worthy adversary may leverage false indicators as decoys. Events examined in isolation are inconclusive but may be relevant for subsequent correlation as context surfaces. The intrusion detection frame of reference where a high volume of generalized security events are harvested and reported to SIEM services for analysis of potential security incidents snowballed into a big data conundrum. The low signal-to-noise ratio in active risk identification stems from fundamental gaps in detection and analysis grammar caused by inadequate time sensitive context to ascertain the polarization of entangled events by time and location. During a post breach forensic analysis drill, one begins with the assumption that actionable evidence exists to discover and establish root cause and modus operandi. In the pre-breach evidence analysis mode, one examines observations that in isolation may be inconclusive, but may become material evidence later, towards a preemptive incident response.

The volume, variety and velocity of events based on broadly scoped pattern matching expressions, stale threat intelligence, inaccurate threat categorization, and/or out-of-date (vintage) rules lead to a high occurrence of inconclusive raw intrusion or anomaly alerts. Context aware filtering and correlation of raw alerts through automated profiling helps triage security events and limit the overhead of manual intervention caused by false assertions of a security incident. The contextual evaluation and relevant risk assessment of a security event before qualifying the indicator as a signal (or noise) is a key function of automation. Automation is a means to manage false positives, and not an elixir that eliminates them altogether.

The Fog of Data

The excessive reliance on monetized threat intelligence (e.g. signature-based rules and reputation lists) from a plurality of data sources without authoritative attribution merely constitutes prima facie evidence. False positives are caused by dependency on anecdotal signatures and fast flux IP addresses, domains, and URLs in cyberspace. Data may be the new oil but is certainly not the center of gravity for threat analytics. Data without attribution of trustworthiness, for context and relevance, is raw, unreliable, and the root cause of false positives. Benchmarking of a security product based on the depth of detection based on threat intelligence causes an evaluation bias. Analytics of voluminous security events (the big data conundrum) generated by untrustworthy threat intelligence will require abductive reasoning and threat pattern recognition that is agnostic to counterbalance data bias. While biased data references may still be credible as independent variables, the germaneness of the information in an analysis to profile and classify risky behaviors requires qualified dependent variables that may refute the threat intelligence and reduce false positives. Unless the threat intelligence is timely, accurate and credible, any remediation action that could automatically intervene and preempt a breach is not a pragmatic policy or security control.

Qualifying a Risk Incident

Detection Tools	• Edge Firewalls • Intrusion Detection Systems (IDS) • Intrusion Prevention Systems (IPS) • Anti-Virus
Volume	• Millions of Daily Alerts • Low Signal to Noise Ratio
Expert Systems	• Analysis of Security Events • Inspecting True/False Positives • Tailing the Real Indicators

Separation of Duties

Network administrators manage the wiring closet where visibility is critical. IT administrators deal with system integrity where timely remediation is crucial. SOC operators are the first responders during a security incident where control is vital. A powerful defense strategy requires key stakeholders to have the visibility and control to remediate in a crisis.

Incident Response

At the root of any incident response process (and strategy) is the capability to harvest core evidence with instrumentation for detection and broad grammar for analysis. Encryption and obfuscation technologies are the Achilles heel of end-to-end trust. The fluidity of bilateral data exchanges poses a unique challenge to grammar-based inspection. The emerging trend in behavioral and contextual analysis requires rethinking the risk model to articulate the complex interactions between the various silos (user, device, application and data objects). Detection (stateful or stateless) is only as reliable as the information that primes the content inspection engine, and analytics is only as accurate as the logic that correlates entangled events. The distribution of events, from indisputable non-threats to the far-right tail of definitive-threats at the extremes, to the high volume of inconclusive gray matter between the extremes, require introspection beyond anomalistic and historic signature interpretation. For effective security, grammar must be a statement of purpose and intent to establish rationale, not anomalous behavior to qualify as a deviation from a pre-established baseline. While machine learning (and implied profiling) is an interesting notion, the diversity and complexity in network, system and device level operations today blurs the differentiation between normal and abnormal to establish a reliable baseline as the frame of reference.

The motives (intent) of a human (user) are far more intricate to comprehend than that of a machine (device). Implicit trust in real time is based on a set of predicates (e.g. multi factor authentication, role-based access controls) that establish a mezzanine level of confidence. Establishing explicit trust in real time requires a collaborative and snapshot decision based on temporal indicators from a multi-part arsenal of detection and analytics methods in a multi-facet stack of security monitors.

Risks are posed by both hierarchical and non-hierarchical interactions between (trusted and untrusted) components. The intrinsic nature of how such interactions occur differ and require appropriate mitigation strategies. Hierarchical security is based on a down-the-stack proactive privilege management, whereas non-hierarchical security requires peer-to-peer inter-component monitors. Hierarchical models tend to be more structured and non-intrusive than the non-hierarchical models (to accommodate legacy, hybrid and pure applications).

The IT Cybersecurity Stack

The IT cybersecurity stack is a three-layer model: Detection, Analytics, and Incident Response.

The detection layer provides traffic examination (with deep packet inspection) to identify threats based on information in packet headers and payload, relying on repository signatures and expressions of well-known (publicized) attack patterns. The rulesets are based on grammar that is predominantly open and extensible to the security stakeholders. Specialized detection grammar is necessary (the gap) to examine scattered dialogs, callbacks, obfuscation, data exchanges, signaling, and volatile actions of malicious applications that occur at distinct stages in the lifecycle of malware.

The Analytics layer began as a compliance-oriented solution for security information and event management (SIEM). The volume, velocity and variety of data led to a "big data" conundrum and the emergence of data analytics to mine, aggregate, normalize and join structured and unstructured information streams for use case driven correlation (e.g. audit, fraud detection, anomaly detection, threat identification). Contrary to the intuitive (inductive, deductive) reasoning of SIEM, threat identification and risk assessment pose a critical (abductive) reasoning challenge (the gap).

The Incident Response layer provides the anticipatory intelligence with visibility and control to SOC operators (the first responders) to manage emergencies in a timely manner to preempt a breach and prevent proliferation of threats. The gaps in the detection and analytics layers lead to onerous false positives and the blind spots that cause catastrophic false negatives.

Mind the Gap

The separation of duties and roles across network administrators, system administrator, field operators, and SOC operators is a crucial factor in early situation awareness and response. The failure to detect activities that provide totality of evidence causes an inability to analyze the observations for relevancy of the evidence and hinders timely response to the security incident. Gap analysis is key to a robust and resilient cybersecurity posture.

Evidence must be harvested from womb to tomb. The network administrators manage access controls in the wiring closet (network silos) that comprise of a plurality of network elements in the enterprise fabric (switches, routers, IDS/IPS, firewall, proxies). The system administrators manage the compute and storage silos (endpoint devices, web/applications/database servers) and are primarily responsible for the configuration and integrity of the respective nodes. The SOC operators are the first responders and deal with security incidents (damage control, forensic analysis, business continuity in a compromised environment). Time is of tremendous essence and relevant information (context) is key to informed decisions.

Role of Expert Systems

Automation serves as an effective means to augment the human in the loop (the eyes) with expert systems (the unmanned engine) to accelerate incident response with fine grained visibility (the glass). Applying the concepts of quantum theory to event-based analytics, one may conclude that entangled events remain highly correlated even if separated by time and location. If you measure the polarization of these entangled events, their properties will be the same. These events are tricky to manipulate because any disturbance causes them to fall out of their quantum state.

Security versus Trust

Security is a control that may be delivered as an aggregation of packaged products, but Trust is a chain that must be bundled as a service. Any logical end to end transaction over cyber is about people, process and product. As products are embodiments of technology, and processes merely enforce established policy statements, end to end trust filters down through people, policy and technology.

- People: Users, Administrators, Unmanned Actors
- Policy: Authentication, Access Controls, Authorization (Roles, Permissions, Privileges)
- Technology: Network Devices, Network Services, Endpoint Services, Connected Devices

The untrustworthy wildcard under the people category is malware – the unmanned actor that uses impersonation or delegation to represent a user.

The policy enforcement point may be in the network fabric and/or the application layer.

Network Devices include network firewalls, intrusion detection or prevention systems and anti-malware gateways. Network Services include security information and event management (SIEM), network flow monitors, and endpoint assessment scanners (i.e. integrity monitoring and verification services). Endpoint Services include anti-virus, host-based intrusion detection systems (HIDS), and runtime integrity monitors. Connected Devices include the Internet of Things (IoT), the controllers, sensors, actuators in Industrial IoT (IIoT), HMI workstations, and brown/greenfield devices in operational technology (OT).

Confluence of Trust

Identity management, in isolation, is not a solution to mitigate a security incident or data breach. An insider or landed threat leverages authentication and authorization through impersonation and/or delegation to evade suspicion. Traditional role-based access controls (RBAC) are required for identity-based admission controls. Implementing RBAC with static and/or dynamic separation of duties and principle of least privilege is tedious and requires process maturity to regulate actions and activities of legitimate users without hindering productivity. Unfortunately, malware on an infected system operates under an assumed (implicit) identity to compromise RBAC.

Beyond RBAC, detecting lateral reconnaissance requires policy controls based on real time flow metrics to identify risky behaviors, suspicious signaling and data exchanges between classified and unclassified silos in a routing fabric that is predominantly secured through subnet and VLAN based zones. Modeling typical workflows based on identity and privileges is harder to achieve for anomaly detection as establishing a trusted baseline is a serious challenge. This approach may lead to false positives and require continuous and ad-hoc recalibration with manual intervention. Attribution of systems (assets) is necessary to define strategic correlation grammar between users, application and data silos in a large enterprise network. Plugging all gaps in vulnerability, patch and compliance management is a cumbersome task for IT as review board cycles are laborious and the volume of exposures published on a regular basis is significant.

Identity Management	• Authentication • Authorization • Access controls • Privilege controls • Password synchronization • Insider threat (activity attribution)
Federated Identity Management	• Access controls to cross-realm applications and services • Brokered identity • Segregation of identity and service providers
Lateral Network Management	• Authoritative user access to network services • Group affiliations and roles • Application identifier • Location • Time • Risk profile (abuse of privilege)
Network Access Management	• Network firewall • Intrusion detection and prevention • Application firewall • Identity based access control • Infection profile (system compromise)
Application Entitlement Management	• Granular authorization and access control • Real time enforcement of logical access control • Externalize security from applications • Integrity profile (operational integrity)
Device Management	• Device identification (immutable) • Device authentication • Supply chain provenance (trust chain) • Tamper resistance (trusted updates, keys, and certificates) • Trust attestation (measured state)
Compliance Management	• Assure auditors of identity-based access controls • Identity based risk management, auditing and enforcement • Trust metrics for incident response

Aggregation of network, flow and endpoint assessments requires integration with an ecosystem of disparate security controls that can augment the IT risk management process with totality of evidence for analysis and inference of risk. While signature and anomaly-based solutions serve a definitive purpose, gaps in detection and analysis due to dynamic flux requires deployment of emerging behavior-based approaches to facilitate in preemptive incident response.

The confluence of trust is an aggregation of assessments based on management of identity, network admission, lateral access, application entitlements, and compliance. Correlation of a plurality of indicators requires intricate grammar based on a join of dependent and independent variables to construct patterns for comparison against an exhaustive set of normal or abnormal behaviors to detect outliers and malicious activities.

Anatomy of a Threat

The anatomy of a threat (or risk) comprises of intricate connections and attribution of trust in the user, code and data. The pathways for connections with unintended consequences are depicted by the dotted lines.

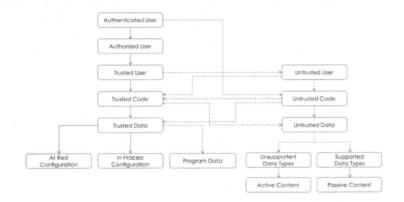

Figure 38: Hierarchy of Trust

Chapter 18

The Epicenter of Cloud Computing

Trust is at the epicenter of Cloud Computing and the single most powerful enabler for cloud migration, and probably even more compelling than promises of savings in capital and operating expenses. Moving data to the cloud is the real tough decision point, not hosting applications in the cloud. Applications are compromised, but it's the data that is lost or stolen. Data whether at rest, in process or in flight is the real asset; the application is merely a virtual asset.

Security is often viewed by many as simply a matter of policies, best practices and processes coupled with multiple layers of disparate point solutions. Trust is much more complicated than user or device identity-based access and authorization, compliance audits based on logs, and file level encryption. Malware can do anything an authenticated user or device can and does not leave a log trail. There is no organic stretch potential in identity aware firewalls. Antivirus is an effective remediation method but was not designed for contextual action correlation. Sandboxes offer reasonable introspection in isolation, but the fundamental problem is that anti-inspection tricks that were conceived for goodness's sake to prevent reverse engineering (code packers, code obfuscation, anti-dumping, anti-trace, anti-emulation, anti-debugging, etc.) are being repurposed by malware for deceit.

The real vulnerability is the hard edge, soft core posture. It is not enough to secure the edge, if you cannot trust the core. The big question then is "how do we define trust?" Trust is fundamentally about "runtime operational integrity" (true measure of ROI for customers). Security is the means; Trust is the end – a dialectic orchestration of multiple security controls. You cannot trust things you cannot measure with certainty and in real environments. The OS platforms today are poorly instrumented for such a purpose. Even allow-lists can be exploited to defeat supply chain provenance with the layers of third-party components and open source commonly being packaged into applications today and the complex software assembly line that delivers the final distribution package. The airplane model is one classic example of good instrumentation as the basis for trust. When you get on a plane and fly at 30,000 feet, you can trust the plane because it is instrumented to assist trained pilots deal with shifts in weather conditions, turbulence, air pockets, etc.

A paradigm shift is necessary to focus on malware's operational footprint rather than the delivery mechanisms alone. Once a system is infected a soft-detection, collaborative analysis and tiered remediation strategy requires a bold new approach and mindset to build an auto pilot for IT services to respond to infections.

While a trust score serves as a measure of trusted security posture as configured, a forensic confidence score is an indicator of trustworthiness of a system as measured. It is non-trivial to assert that any piece of software can be trusted unconditionally at all times because of runtime entropy, and the possibility that vulnerabilities and exploits could be discovered at any stage of the software run cycle. Unfortunately, in software, supply chain provenance is not reliable (in the absolute sense), because of the fluidity and dynamic bindings that occur during execution. There is a high level of entropy in an applications response to data inputs. Tightly coupled systems are solid, the cloud platform is fluid, and applications are gaseous (loosely coupled and exhibit high entropy). The attack surface at the application layer is too wide for comfort without a means to instrument and measure trustworthiness.

Threat Vectors

The old-fashioned threat vectors were merely scratching at the surface. Emerging advanced malware is poised for attack in depth exploiting users, devices, processes and systems alike, requiring a measured response by the security industry. This can only be achieved through "security intelligence collaboration" and amplifying the power of disparate security solutions in the Enterprises arsenal to better identify and respond to advanced threats. From a customer's standpoint, it does not matter which deployed products contributed intelligence to the timely diagnosis, just that the threats are caught before there is irreversible damage. Threat information sharing is the vehicle to build a grid for advanced threat detection.

The layered security model with an arsenal of security controls has significantly improved security between tightly coupled physical systems. However, systems are now becoming loosely coupled, virtualized and distributed (device to device, device to cloud). This shifting of the tectonic plates in emerging data centers and edge clouds clearly signals the necessity to rethink the security divide between access controls, intrusion prevention, infection detection and remediation – in that order. Given the status quo with regards to cyber-attacks and data breaches, infection detection remains the weakest link. Access controls achieve a very specific purpose by allowing or denying access based on a policy statement. Intrusion prevention solutions have kept fair pace with intruders – but are always lagging by one move – the next move the intruder will make. You can read the hacker's traffic, but can you read the hacker's mind? Antivirus provides a pragmatic remediation method to "clean up the mess" from a standpoint of achieving business continuity in a compromised system. But the one area that still needs work is infection diagnosis – the gaps that can still cause fatal data breaches, not because of IT negligence, but due to lack of protection valves, situational threat intelligence and awareness. Throwing more security analysts at big data is not a long-term strategy – it only emboldens Hacktivists to improvise as the haystack grows … and it most likely will.

Security analytics for threat identification and classification for remediation requires recalibration of security controls to analyze the behavior (and response) of systems under normal and abnormal conditions. Risk based correlation logic to identify the operational state (mind) of a system based on behavior is an early indicator of possible compromise of the integrity of the system (perhaps an application gone rogue). Instead of looking for needles in big data, the focus needs to shift to "inconspicuous events". SIEM solutions have predominantly focused on correlation logic based on business processes (for regulatory compliance – a necessary component of security) but have not scaled to dealing with coordination centric malware with time and location sensitive fuses. Active event correlation has greater synergy with life cycle models of threats, compared to passive log correlation which works effectively with business logic models. It is easier to describe a business process than the anatomy of a threat from an audit or rule administration perspective to security stakeholders who have to establish and enforce policies.

Why Security Needs to Handle Changeups

In baseball, the change-up is a pitch that arrives much slower to the plate. The reduced speed coupled with a deceptive delivery style is intended to confuse the batter's timing. In similar style, low-and-slow threats are the slow-ball of Cyber Attacks.

Security over the past decades has relied heavily on access controls and IT processes as the fundamental approach to a strong defense. As attackers became more sophisticated, access controls proved ineffective. Identity is not the core problem. Detection techniques that relied exclusively on instant algorithms circled around commonly abused (or web used) protocols like HTTP need to be re-purposed to handle slow techniques that are crafted for multistage deceptive delivery and a targeted evasive mode of operation. The industry has focused on how malware looks, rather than how malware operates. That must change.

In the emerging security equation, big data is the new reality, and the old tool chest is inadequate to deal with the low signal to noise ratio of low and slow attacks. The hard-edge soft-core model is tilted towards outsider threats and does not address the insider threat and post compromise landscape. Malware identifies people as the asset and is immune to access controls. Current vulnerability, configuration, compliance and patch management solutions focus on and highlight the weak spots (what could happen) but do not deal with and identify the blind spots (what is already happening). All of the above gaps work in the Hacktivists favor today.

Reversing the chess board requires multiple initiatives including making the window of exposure bidirectional (so it works both ways), making the attacker equally vulnerable, engaging in hot pursuit instead of passive resistance, and a counter reconnaissance on the intended victim to strengthen the immune system. Risk aggregation and correlation with multi-dimensional integrity metrics to engage attack preparation and post infection behaviors requires tenaciously calibrated network and on-device sensors. A collective set of strategic assessments (interactions focused, inspection of operation sequences), net assessments (outcomes forecast, threats equate to different levels of explicit damage on each victim), and continuous scoring of users (social and professional), devices (managed and unmanaged), services (web servers), applications, and transactions are required for a collaborative counter offensive.

The VERIS A4 Threat Model eloquently describes agents (external, internal, partners), actions (malware, hacking, social, misuse, physical, environmental), assets (servers, user devices, people), and attributes (confidentiality, integrity). People are clearly the carbon layer (social animals, gullible). Computers are simple to program and behave in predictable ways, people are complicated. The threat chain is an action sequence beginning with the user (agent), malware (actor), service (exploit), device (victim) and finally the data (contraband). The user is the weakest link in this chain. Hacktivists therefore solicit the user as the entry point (through email attachments, social networking, drive-by-downloads, web links). Malware uses an arsenal of obfuscation techniques (binary, API, control flow, just-in-time unpacking and re-packing, time-bombs, suicide-code). While static analysis decompiles and analyzes the potential of the binary itself (logical structure, flow and data content), dynamic analysis profiles actions at runtime (unpacked, perhaps partially) in a sandbox. Risk correlation analyzes benign actions at runtime and maps the action sequences to malicious patterns.

The landscape of emerging threats is wide and open from a remote attacker to a co-resident attacker in multi-tenant infrastructures (comparable to urban warfare). General purpose north-south security mindset is a fallacy (entry points are ubiquitous). Retrofitting legacy access control methods to block threats is ineffective (execution versus access control). The long overdue east-west security lacks instrumentation for threat recognition (in the soft core).

What is the motive, opportunity and means for a cybercriminal? The motive includes financial, activism and cyber terrorism by private and/or state sponsors. The vehicle of opportunity is easily available through drive-by-downloads, web links, email attachments, documents (pdf, ppt, xls, rar), and social networking. The means are abundant from users (gullible, renegades) to the lack of collaboration between security controls (the inability to connect the dots until a breach has occurred). While a fortified defense is essential with a hard edge of layered security controls, a counter-offense strategy requires smarter instrumentation to deal with threats that have evaded the defenses (airgaps, ant-holes) to reduce the post-infection, pre-damage window of exposure and make it difficult for attackers to obfuscate behavior in the soft core.

As Enterprises worldwide upgrade their data center and end-user workstation infrastructures to deal with big data, virtualization based on-demand services, and Bring Your Own Device (BYOD) initiatives, the security paradigm will require a change-up. The promise of lowering IT (capital and operating) expenses will raise the bar to achieve higher operational efficiencies with automated threat analytics. Security cannot scale up (or out) with compute, network and storage unless the mindset shifts from a signature-centric, north-south orientation to an active introspection-centric model that address east-west co-resident threats especially in emerging multi-tenant workloads. Automated identification and classification of imminent threats based on active (runtime) intelligence, post infection risk assessment models based on outcomes (cost of breach) for early warning, and remediation of coordinated and targeted attacks will drive innovation in IT services. The successful adoption of emerging Software Defined Networking (SDN) in a loosely coupled and fluid ecosystem demands a tightly coupled immune system to actively monitor the integrity of applications, flows and transactions. While next generation defensive strategies focus on identifying malware delivery mechanisms in a controlled environment (sandbox or virtual execution) an offensive strategy observes how coordination-centric malware operates on intended (real) targets within the target (real) environment with corroborative evidence and forensic confidence to reduce false positives and negatives.

Attack Lifecycle Modeling

Every form of traditional warfare has used a bag of age-old tactics and strategies. The defender builds watchtowers, deeper moats, and higher walls to observe and block the intruders and protect the castle and the crown jewels. The enemy then employs deceptive (and perhaps unfair) means with Trojan horses or a renegade on the inside to breach the apparently invincible defenses. And so it is with Cyber Warfare.

Cyber Attacks do not happen, they are caused. Traditional legacy and emerged security solutions such as next-generation anti-virus, network firewalls, intrusion detection/prevention systems operate based on signatures, protocol anomalies or virtual execution in a sandbox to monitor threats and attacks. However, once the target system becomes infected or compromised, these technologies have been proven ineffective in the protection of the systems and prevention of data breaches or service disruptions. Emerging attacks exhibit a low and slow mode of operation and are signature-less to evade traditional defensive methods. Further, these technologies underestimate the versatility of today's hackers.

A significant metric that relates to the ineffectiveness of current security controls is the high rate of false positives and negatives in the detection of threats. False positives are unproductive and reduce operating capacity in data centers. False negatives lead to the bypass of security controls and compromise of the target systems and services. Signature based approaches are vulnerable to improvised attacks staged on meticulously targeted systems.

The proliferation of applications (business, social networking and gaming software) in Enterprise and cloud computing ecosystems has significantly increased the attack surface and window of exposure. Application runtime operational integrity is a critical factor in building end-to-end trust from device to service. The proliferation of unmanaged devices such as mobile smart phones and Bring Your Own Device (BYOD) policies in Enterprise network environments have increased the risk of advanced coordinated threats.

Threat assessment has predominantly focused on the footprint of attacks. As the footprints are becoming significantly smaller, their detection is getting increasingly harder. Emphasis on the visible footprint has resulted in lack of attention to the tactics beneath the footprint. Attacks are no longer single stage isolated events detectable on the wire at the packet level. They require interpretation of context and intent to eliminate false positives and false negatives. The emerging forms of targeted and coordinated attacks have evolved into multistage coordinated events exhibiting benign intent at the surface.

The life cycle of a cyber-attack mimics the life cycle of an infection in the human body, beginning with the victim contracting the disease-causing germ through a communicable medium – egg download. The infection is then transmitted and spreads to other individuals in the vicinity – peer to peer propagation. Once the germ has infected the victim, the damage potential increases depending on the strength of the immune systems – command and control communication. The disease gradually exploits the weakness of the immune systems, harms vital organs, and becomes fatal – data exfiltration. Effective intervention requires meticulous diagnosis of the signs and symptoms to diagnose the disease correctly and in a timely manner to administer appropriate treatment – manual remediation. The human body implements an automated counter-offensive mechanism releasing matching (specific) antibodies (proteins) to fight the antigen (virus). And almost as a means to boost the immune system for increased resilience, preventive interventions (vaccines) are required to monitor and correlate dysfunctions (anomalies or abnormal behaviors) in the system (human or computer models) – automated remediation.

Attack Lifecycle Modeling of cyber threats is necessary to strengthen the IT immune system in emerging virtualization and cloud-based data centers where the attack surface and window of exposure are significantly higher than the industry has previously dealt with. The low and slow threats that manage to circumvent traditional north-south hard edges and navigate east-west across the soft cores inside the perimeter can be detected by analyzing and mapping events to an attack profile rather than millions of high entropy signatures and IP deny-lists. The intrinsic nature of building a life cycle model renders a quantitative and qualitative measure of confidence level in the assessment of perceived threats based on an evidence chain (or warrant), thereby significantly lowering false positives and negatives. Hacktivists have demonstrated their uncanny prowess in morphing signatures to evade detection by traditional security check-posts.

Only attack lifecycle modeling offers an adaptive mechanism that is scalable and can generate appropriate matching criteria to identify threats forms (mutations) based on context and intent. The signature footprints are infinite, but the underlying modus operandi is finite which makes the threat model highly extensible. Just like an antibody which must recognize and match with the antigen to interlock (i.e. the key must match the lock) a behavior-based threat correlation model eliminates noise and latches with the signal to reduce false positives and negatives. The accuracy of threat identification and evidence chain is extremely crucial to focus valuable IT cycles on the real risks and provide both visibility and control of the operational integrity of complex interconnected workloads in today's large and shared computing infrastructures without simply shifting the onus of meticulously configuring firewall, intrusion detection/prevention, and anti-virus rules to defend against unidentified threats to information security stakeholders. Unlike network access controls which are based on business logic and processes, threat management does not naturally lend itself to a discrete and comprehensive security posture characterization thereby making security orchestration a difficult mission for any organization. It is time for a counter-offensive.

Convergence of Network and Security

The convergence of networks and security appears to be a very logical and rational epoch. Networking was invented for connectivity, or communications, between distributed entities (perhaps geographical at first, but later evolved into loose coupling between a consumer and provider). Security, in network parlance, meant "integrity" of the messaging channel/media, where no wiretaps or sniffing could compromise the data in transit. These days, security means protection from "border-less" crime-ware (bots, trojans, spyware, malware, impersonation of application protocols, etc.) across the intranet and extranet, implying that the malicious user and/or application may exemplify diverse forms and originate from almost anywhere (insider and outsider threats).

That makes one deliberate on the genesis of the security breach – where it all began, at an endpoint (like a stream that flows into a river or a river that flows into the ocean). One would imagine building a levy or dam at the point of influx to be a rational choice rather than draining the ocean.

The seven-layer OSI protocol stack is a pretty robust piece of machinery. TCP/IP has served us very well in spite of all the uncontrolled activities transiting up and down the communications stack. The network was not designed for end-to-end application security. The semantics of the application layer protocols (and services) are clearly beyond the scope of the underlying network. Bump-in-the-wire solutions evolved over the past decades as an overlay on the network, but as the security threats evolved, these solutions have become hard-to-scale choke points and single points of failure.

One needs to take a step back at the network and treat it as "strictly transport" – or plumbing infrastructure. Can this transport become a channel to additionally relay trust between peer-to-peer entities? It certainly could. Extending the model of trust to include user and calling/called application, using the network in the role it was designed for, i.e. transport, offers a paradigm shift in fixing the security problem in a holistic way.

Security cannot be completely decoupled from applications, as tempting as it may be. Networked applications are part of the problem and as such applications must be held accountable to participate proactively in end-to-end security (through integrated top-down provisioning of entitlements and event logs for external audit and compliance reports).

The network can facilitate mutual trust between applications, without being expected to deliver total enforcement of security. The network trust can be complemented with additional security plug-ins in the peer applications (in-band, and transparent to the network). The network becomes a baseline for legacy applications that were not designed with security on the agenda. Ultimately, the crown jewels that are being protected are not servers or applications, but the "data". The data is always secure; it is the application(s) and underlying protocols which access this data that may be insecure. Network elements in the plumbing (switches, routers, firewalls, etc.) can derive valuable trust indicators from the network at line speed, to become facilitators of extended security.

The network datagram operates analogous to regular mail. The post office delivers the mail simply because someone deposited a package with the correct postage. The recipient ("to" name and address) is required to exercise reasonable judgment in inspecting the "from" name and address before opening the package. In network jargon, the network is the mailman, and the receiving application is the recipient. The network inspects and transports based on trust (no ticking sounds, X-ray scan is clean, sniff test passed) and the peer application makes the final network-savvy decision to consume the delivered packet. Fair is fair. If the network and applications must evolve to achieve security objectives, so be it.

An endpoint-based security supplicant, serving as a thin bump-in-the-stack below the network layer (packet filter), can embed user and application identification watermarks (based on multi-factor authentication and application allow-lists) negotiated during a secure authentication session with a centralized policy distribution server (authentication and authorization server). Any network element, subscribing to the policy server (push model in the control path), can process and honor the security watermarks (labels) to drop or forward the packet. Trust is baked into the packet and designed for high-speed packet processing in the data path (analogous to an ATM switch, with a preconfigured location/offset in the datagram to realize implementation efficiencies on hardware/ASIC). The current approach of deriving context based on application content with a bump-in-the-wire does not scale and is not easily extensible. The nature and intensity of zero-day attacks are overwhelming. As an alternative to reactive deny-listing and signature/content-based heuristics, embedding security context in the flow with an endpoint-based security supplicant, and inspecting the security posture at a mid-stream network appliance is stateless and scalable.

Trusted packets are the building blocks of secure networks. The network may be flat today; however the network security domain remains hierarchical in nature. Vulnerabilities and exploits exist across the entire stack, the application layer, the transport layer, and the network layer. The degree of trust between peer applications is a cumulative measure of the dynamic trust of the platform, application and authenticated/domain (managed) user and should be relayed baked into every packet, rather than being bolted onto a remote stack (proxy or deep packet inspection appliance) along the flow without the trailing trust indicators available at the source. The endpoint (host) and the network (appliance) must enforce security in close collaboration through communicable and authoritative trust. The high throughput low latency expectations on network routers and switches require that context-based inspection engines operate at line speed. An application allow-list based signature approach offers higher hardware efficiencies than a heuristics-based application protocol recognition approach.

Security labels baked into packets can traverse through existing plumbing and network elements seamlessly, without violating the TCP/IP protocol, address/port translations, and encryption (SSL tunnels). Routers and switches in the wiring closet may be optionally upgraded to collaborate with the endpoint security supplicants or remain passive and delegate the security function to a bump-in-the-wire inline appliance as an incremental network enhancement in front of or behind a traditional external (DMZ) or internal firewall.

This approach offers a flexible, agile, extensible, Intranet and Internet application allow-listing centric approach to user identity and application trust-based network admission and access controls; with standards based multi-vendor interoperability across ASIC, FPGA, COTS and open-source security platforms. It levels the playing field for host (bump-in-the-stack) and network (bump-in-the-wire) centric enforcement methodologies to work in concert with intelligence sharing. Trust association embedded in every packet is a perfect elixir for route redundancy in meshed core networks and associated complexities introduced in context sensitive deep packet inspection engines in terms of stateful failover for high availability. A stateless flow management paradigm for network-based access control also facilitates in load balancing and management of solicited flows based on a policy-based control flow.

The convergence of networks and security, as the network evolves into a super-computer of sorts, requires tighter collaboration between network admission controls and network access controls. The fundamental flaw in Network Admission Controls (NAC) was the mindset that a standalone solution was the only pragmatic approach, with access controls in the plumbing or admission controls at the endpoint. Instead of a standalone solution bolted on at a remote stack somewhere in the plumbing or at a multitude of host/guest (OS) platforms, a rational bifurcation of roles is required based on a combination of host-based bump-in-the-stack and a network appliance-based bump-in-the-wire. Heuristics and digital foot-print centric content inspection are reactive and must be reincarnated as a proactive application allow-list based trust centric paradigm. Building security into the network, real or virtual, requires baking in dynamic trust indicators into every packet based on an authoritative and cumulative assertion of trust and a centralized management system. The network may be flat; however the network security (problem) domain is hierarchical and therefore the policy decision logic is conceivably distributed. As core computing in today's high-speed networks gradually evolves into a distributed model with dumb endpoints and plumbing, a paradigm shift is required at the core networking level to relay intelligence for security enforcement at multiple points of inspection, namely at switches, routers, firewalls, and peer-to-peer applications. Security cannot be decoupled from the application itself, because the primary asset being protected is the data and applications which access such data must be secured. That defines the convergence of Data Leakage Protection (DLP) and application level two-way (mutual) trust as an integral part of NAC. The network was conceived primarily as a transport (messaging) vehicle and is neither the cause nor contributor to the security threats at hand, whose origins may trace back to malicious or badly engineered applications. Therefore the network cannot be expected to enforce total end-to-end security unilaterally.

The Power of Observation

The move from "log correlation" to "behavioral risk" requires a paradigm shift. The first generation of cybersecurity solutions leveraged the power of "logs". This was based on the credence that ad-hoc events once captured and preserved may be correlated in the future to provide historical evidence. Logs are valuable for technical support, troubleshooting and audits. The log centric model was designed to fulfil compliance requirements and verify security controls implemented for access management.

The proliferation of malware in the past decade led to the second generation of cybersecurity solutions that shifted the spotlight onto "files". This was based on the notion that malware is an incarnation of a file and is transmitted over the wire through application layer protocols (e.g. web, email, file transfer/shares) analogous to a communicable human disease through air, food, water or body fluids. The pathological examination of the file led to static and dynamic analysis (analogous to blood/urine tests, x-rays, CT scans) on a bench analyzer, to generate a diagnostics report for a prognosis by a specialist to forecast likely outcome. The file is the piece of information on which a conclusion is drawn. Then a vaccine or antibiotic is manufactured to preempt or treat the disease (and another signature is born). But alas, just like viruses and bacteria, malware developed resistance and mutated like its human counterpart.

The realization that high profile security and data breaches continue to intensify and proliferate led to the third generation of cybersecurity solutions that are prevalent today leveraging statistical learning and pattern recognition for detection of "anomalous activities". This approach establishes a baseline of order and then detects deviations from the baseline (outliers) to identify disorders to provide early intervention for entropy management on an episodic basis. An anomaly may be the presence of unexpected files (or installed applications) in a file system, configuration settings that violate best practices, activities that exceed normal thresholds, or exhibit uncommon patterns. However, this approach does not discover the modus operandi of emerging advanced persistent threats (APTs) to share actionable threat intelligence.

Today, the ground reality of the situation is that systems may be infected, and networks already compromised due to a plurality of factors – from increasing complexity of the ecosystem, fuzzy perimeters, outdated IT processes, unmanaged devices, dynamic workloads (virtual instances), insider threats and a cybercrime syndicate of equal strength, means and economic motives. This requires the fourth generation of cybersecurity solutions with a paradigm shift to "behaviors". Behaviors are continuous observations for risk analysis to build a hypothesis that facilitates in the discovery of otherwise hidden threat indicators based on real evidence. With this approach, a data-driven model provides certainty metrics of undesirable outcomes. This is a preventive, pre-emptive, and proactive approach like a healthy diet (policies to control entitle-ments), exercise (processes) and wellness visits (continuous monitoring) in the healthcare arena.

Smart observations require sound instrumentation and real time collab-oration with security solutions deployed at the perimeter and in the soft core. This serves as a force multiplier to augment the human in the loop with auto-mation based expert systems.

Security Essentials for Enterprise Risk Management

The core foundation of cyber security needs to be reinforced from the exposed limitations of legacy controls that have outlived the compliance and signa-ture-based paradigm. The new paradigm for Enterprise Risk Management (ERM) is based on real evidence from active behavior recognition, reducing false positives (the fog) through automation that augments human-level IQ, real-time threat intelligence sharing to enrich context, and partnerships that streamline workflow. The challenges posed include processes (in-house versus outsourced), overheads (metadata and activity log retention) and the emerged ecosystems (cloud orchestration and software defined networking).

Incidence response requires both situation awareness and tiered remedi-ation actions for proportional response. Workflow is task-oriented and requires real-time alert correlation, activity log analysis, traffic capture and analysis, and suspect file detonation for security analysts to perform deep-dive evidence anal-ysis to reach decisive conclusions. The variety of specialized multivendor secu-rity tools, a frictionless integration surface and ease of use with an economy of clicks is essential for total remediation at the 'compromised network' and 'infected system' level to restore normalcy and trustworthiness of operations. The probability and impact determine the urgency and consequences respec-tively, while the relevance of the evidentiary chain of data points (indicators) and visualization dashboards determine the 'velocity of decision', a key metric in a sustainable cyber security posture.

Actionable information sharing about advanced threats requires harvest-ing of information through honeypots and monkeynets, discovery of unknown unknowns and verification of malicious actors for qualification of risks before any information may be deemed reliable. Attackers could hinder any information sharing framework with decoys (noise) thereby diminishing returns unless the framework is selective. This requires a behavior recognition model that is differentiated and complementary to signature and exploit centric approaches.

Real time collaboration is required for actionable information sharing as the half-life of information is low because of the rapid flux in leading indicators (e.g. IP addresses, domain names, signatures). That imposes stringent time-sensitive requirements on security controls to be dynamic and adaptive. Information exchange is a strategy that an Enterprise may adopt based on an anonymization policy for liability protection. Security vendors must support mechanisms based on an open standard to export and import threat information across controls.

Automation is a means to achieve a balance in the ecosystem with expert systems. Observing Moore's law, does exponential increase in memory and computation capacity equate to faster decisions and accurate conclusions? Machine learning is a science wherein machines reach human-level IQ without explicit programming. While an extensive volume and variety of information harvested through continuous learning and non-volatile machine memory may facilitate data retention and processing, human decisions are derived by a complex calculus of intuitive reasoning, critical thinking and emotional IQ. The influence of a plurality of dependent variables (such as environmental, circumstantial, political, social, geographical) that alter status quo and impact human decision logic require careful contemplation of outcomes. At least in the foreseeable future, human vigilance and machine learning are required as a collaborative model for resilience against cyber threats.

Historically, security has always been an afterthought and cost center. The gasoline engine for powered motor cars was invented in 1876. Airbags were invented a century later in the mid-1970s. Many design and process improvements occur through a series of mishaps and lessons learned. The history of the Internet began in the 1980s – the Internet of Things is still in its pre-teen years. The proliferation of Internet enabled applications and services on the 'information highway' have outpaced policies and processes to safely harness the power of a borderless and fluid cyberspace. As security practitioners scramble to define a sensible strategy for cyber security, the roles and responsibilities of the board, the CEO, the CIO, and the CISO are critical to formulate a plan and budget to counter the damage potential of a complacent posture. Security is a risk center that impacts the fundamental economics associated with operational integrity in a compromised environment, workflow disruptions and recovery costs. A day in the life of a cyber-security first responder hinges on evidence-based reality, velocity of response and active adversary vigilance. Achieving this goal requires a careful rethinking of policies, processes and technologies for broad and synergetic standards-based controls.

Cybersecurity at the Cusp

The ongoing cyber security debate is at a critical crossroad. While hackers and cyber bullies undoubtedly have the industry in their cross hairs, the industry must respond with concrete actions to achieve core objectives outlined in the cyber threat information sharing initiative (2015) proposed by the US Government. Playing victim is not a solution. Now private industry leaders have the opportunity to work with the Government towards a long-term solution. Cyber threats impact public and private sectors, consumers and enterprises alike.

The executive order lays a clear framework for an early warning system across sectors (horizontal and vertical). The federal intelligence agencies have the capability to serve as the trust broker. The public-private nexus is a necessary alliance to define a grass-roots strategy to fight cybercrime. Information sharing, in spirit and in depth, based on anonymization and tokenization of appropriate data for legitimate evidence analysis is necessary to serve a greater public good. Restoring consumer confidence in the digital era requires adoption of a "need to share" paradigm – a far cry from the "need to know" mindset. To "join the dots" industry must "share the dots" to overcome the information deficit that is the root cause of cyber-attack proliferation. As the wise African proverb goes - "If you want to go fast, walk alone. If you want to go far, walk together". Legislators must now acknowledge that cybercrime syndicates have already gained an unfair advantage with dual-use technology. Only innovations in technology that profile and analyze malicious behaviors, in real time and on patient zero, stand a chance to change the status quo for future generations against advanced and targeted attacks.

Legislation is a firm indicator that both technology and market-demand are driving the decision logic apparatus towards action. Today, where cyber security unpleasantly stands, it is an exotic cocktail of retrofitted products, breaking news of data breaches that compromise consumer information at large enterprises, and covert post breach investigations without transparency. In this fog of cyberwar, how can one shape a meaningful roundtable conversation on information sharing that includes a plurality of contextual evidence and auto-mated analytics to amplify the risk indicators? Data breaches are a direct con-sequence of hard to configure security controls and hard to scale IT processes. That points the finger fair and square at the lack of effective instrumentation and processes to defend against the adversary's arsenal.

What IT knows keeps the process on its toes; what IT does not know is what makes the process fail. IT is solving a "minimum information" puzzle without a hint, playing a Hangman game with critical assets. With enough wrong guesses, you are slowly hanging the asset. The hackers have already drawn the gallows before the game begins. The level of "network hygiene", on a frugal in-house budget, and outsourced IT make small businesses an easy target, mid markets a soft target, and large enterprises a value target for cyber criminals. Today, hackers thrive because of indecision and blind trust of security stake-holders on products without a robust process for continuous monitoring. The framework and benchmark are inadequate, to measure cyber resiliency, to counter the lack of visibility that administrators in the network, security and cyber operations center have to deal with, for effective surveillance, investiga-tions and timely remediation to manage risks. The signature and knowledge based reactive mindset must change. A situational awareness based artificial intelligence that beats natural lapses in human oversight, is required to reinforce a zero-tolerance approach.

Effective frameworks will require representation by the next generation of innovative security researchers and industry incumbents. Wider participation is required to understand the depth and scope of the emerging challenges posed by IT processes in small to large enterprises, supply chain blind spots, outsourcing and offshoring. On current course any company is just a hop away, from a disgruntled employee with a grudge or a partner who is the weak link, from compromise and/or data breach. The ecosystem is complex, and geography is history – attacks can be orchestrated from the opposite side of the planet by a team of incentivized and motivated professionals – remote is virtually local. Thinking inside the fence requires CISOs to accept these realities to identify the common denominator to design a strategy for cyber protection.

CISOs must baseline on what has worked and what has not in order to play the "observer role" that provides checks and balances for effective supervision. That is where the solution begins with a clear separation of duties between the CIO and CRO (Chief Risk Officer). Standalone security products by themselves are just an embodiment of a technology. Point solutions are just foot soldiers fighting the battle. What is the cause? What is the desired outcome? What is the strategy? Who is in charge to execute the plan (policies)? The key to success is a process that provides high assurance that policies are enforceable and verifiable with minimal human effort. The execution of any modern cyber resilient process will require trusted instrumentation that overcomes human oversight and errors in judgment at close encounters – the one that came close to deadly impact.

As in any global war, both defense and offense will be required to achieve a decisive outcome. Where reliable information was generally harvested through field operatives (or informers) behind enemy lines, in cyber security parlance that is difficult to achieve. Therefore, information must be harvested internally within the "red zone of defense". That requires smart cyber-ready instrumentation that is unfortunately inadequate on networked systems and devices. Compromised systems comprise the 'last mile' of an attack; the 'first mile' is outside-in field intelligence assembled from trusted data sources. Between these mileposts are IT processes that were designed with access management in mind, not entropy management. There are two response options available: the 'days after harm', or the 'days before damage'. A compromised system is the key indicator of a threat in play. So security first responders have to anchor and drill down on the dot signals. The status-quo in device instrumentation is designed for performance and compliance management, and not to measure runtime operational integrity. Instrumentation to deal with coordination-centric threats will require a common definition of key risk indicators. There is asymmetric urban warfare in cyber space; the 'needle in the haystack' at the hard edge is now a 'cat among the pigeons' in the soft core. Isolated security controls increase the entropy of systems and the fear, uncertainty and doubt (FUD) that comes with it.

Cybersecurity for Critical Infrastructure

Cyber threats and vulnerabilities pose likely and imminent degrees of risk to the critical infrastructure grid which includes facilities, supervisory control and data acquisition systems (SCADA) and field devices. The intricate network architecture of the smart grid is exposed to hidden risks posed by interconnected heterogeneous devices from multiple vendors, integrated open source and commercial off-the-shelf (COTS) components, and minimum (or lack of) supply chain cyber hygiene. The advent of bring your own device (relays, breakers, air conditioning, water heaters, pumps, thermostats, chargers, batteries, remote terminal units, programmable logic controllers, wired/ wireless telemetry, etc.) and remote access mechanisms for data access and control increase volatility and unpredictability in the loosely coupled eco-system. Upstream signaling and transmission from end user devices to servers expands the staging surface for attackers. The separation of duties between operation technology (OT) and information technology (IT) is a contextual gap between focus on reliability and availability versus security and vulnerability management.

Regulations and standards, proposed by North American Electric Reliability Corporation (NERC), Federal Energy Regulatory Commission (FERC) and National Institute of Standards and Technology (NIST), such as Critical Infrastructure Protection (CIP Version 5) and the Cybersecurity Capability Maturity Model (C2M2) establish guidelines to enhance compliance and security. While compliance may reduce risks, compliance is not an assurance of security and does not eliminate all residual risks because audit checklists lag security punch lists due to dynamic flux and evolution of threat vectors.

The traditional strategy of a multi-layer defense with security controls geared towards protections requires complementary and continuous monitoring as a checkpoint for risk aversion and zero tolerance. Excessive reliance on whitelisting and threat data, through intelligence sharing between intelligences agencies, public and private industry causes attribution bias, diagnosis deficit, and concerns about loss of privacy and anonymity. Proactive penetration testing and vulnerability scans in utility grids (bulk power systems, distribution systems, field and control systems, upstream devices) may be disruptive to normal operations and put systems at unnecessary risk.

Coordinated cyber-attacks on utility grids are directed towards sabotage, disruption and ransom rather than theft of intellectual property. Landed malware (delivered as a malicious file attachment or hyperlink by email, through social networking, on a website or a USB device) uses lateral reconnaissance to scan and harvest information, enables attackers through a backdoor for remote command and control, and erases crucial evidence of traceability. Detection of advanced persistent threats requires alerting and reporting capabilities based on real time monitoring of network traffic and flow metrics, signaling integrity in loosely coupled ecosystem, and data exchanges between tiered silos for timely intervention and mitigation. Network device, system and application logs that are generated based on manual configuration of rules are prone to misconfiguration, human error and undiscovered exploits. Further, insider threats posed by authenticated and authorized malicious actors (disgruntled employees, compromised credentials, or physical intrusion to a facility) are a unique challenge in detection of abuse of privilege through behavior analysis, without requiring a cumbersome manual configuration to establish a reliable and trustworthy baseline reference of operational integrity.

A security control (statement of policy) is a collaborative effort between the policy maker and the decision maker, to facilitate in the detection of threats and risks to a business process or operation, to enable mitigation actions to isolate the damaged asset and, to restore normalcy of asset functions for business continuity. This requires a holistic end-to-end approach to build resiliency through strategic systems and network design for fault tolerance based on asset redundancy (active/passive failover model of operation controls) and elimination of single points of operational failure. Identification of asset and impact to qualify activities is critical for early risk awareness and proportional response.

Healthcare Principles and IT Security

Applying the principles of healthcare to IT security is really a good analogy in the sense that the problems and solutions (or lack thereof) have similarities. The IT patient is really the "living" application (and not the machine – which is a passive bystander – guilt by association).

Steroids: Applications are designed by engineers who never really have security on their agenda when designing and implementing solutions. The emphasis is on performance and features. That's like running on Steroids, without contemplating about future consequences.

Aging: The human body's defense system grows weaker over time – a natural aging process. Applications grow old and wither eventually, as new forms of attacks emerge that are alien to its constitution. Applications could be reengineered (like plastic or bypass surgery) to some extent after which even those procedures exhibit diminishing returns, and then you start over using a new language and operating system.

Immunizations: Newborns are immunized as they enter the cruel world outside the womb. This is our scientific sense offering protection in the wild – until the body's natural defenses ramp up. That is where one could argue that applications do not get smarter by themselves over time (self-defending software?). They are deployed with an immunity level pre-established at birth by the engineers. They are later immunized through patch management based on exposures to emerging forms of infections.

Regular Checkups: It is prudent advice to have regular checkups to keep your blood, heart, and arteries well-tuned. What is regular? That depends on factors such as history, heredity, and habits. A younger person may require an annual visit to the physician, a person with Type 2 diabetes may require a sugar check once a day – depends on the stage of diabetes. Applications need to be inspected depending on their likelihood of being infected, based on vulnerability, patch level, configuration compliance, etc.

Lifestyle Choices: We know that old habits die hard, and you cannot teach the old dog new tricks. Lifestyle changes can significantly improve the quality of health (no one promises immortality). Following common sense guidelines enforced by manual or automated processes can go a long way in improving application security – with more emphasis on design and code reviews, testing for compliance criteria, etc. These measures would probably slow down the release train, but the outcome is security baked into applications. Just like automatic flight control systems and satellites have made airline travel safer, with all due respect to trained and qualified pilots, application frameworks need to evolve to automatically provide security safeguards in application development and execution.

Diet Control: Our body is attacked by what we eat and what we breathe. We have no options on the breathing cycles, but we have a choice on eating wisely. What if a restaurant asks me for my cholesterol and blood pressure before taking my order? It certainly would violate my constitutional rights and freedoms. But is it not for my own good? What if I cancel my order after it arrives because my informed re-assessment of the meal indicates that it is too salty for my blood pressure, or too sweet for my Diabetes? If an "access control" mechanism determines that one or both parties (users or applications) in a transaction may not be trustworthy, should it block such a transaction in spite of initial consent by the parties based on a rational assessment of the consequences?

Insurance: Who pays the bills? Isn't this the heart breaker! Healthcare and IT-care are considered cost centers. No one regards them as profit centers. We don't exactly hear employers announce how productive their employees have become with the new company-paid health insurance plan, or CIOs/CISOs proclaim how much their revenue increased last quarter because they installed that next-generation firewall.

Cybersecurity for Healthcare

The healthcare industry is undergoing a radical reform from HIPAA to HITECH with the passage of legislation to (a) impose civil and criminal penalties on willful neglect, and (b) adoption of Electronic Health Records (EHI) with implications on security of electronic Protected Health Information (ePHI) across the supply chain including providers and business associates. These two key provisions will drive how CIOs and CISOs in the healthcare industry must develop processes and policies for compliance and enforcement.

While a policy, by any standard, is merely a stipulation of conditions and actions to address a situation, processes require a series of enforceable steps, that are repeatable, to achieve measurable and desired outcomes. The paradigm shift in healthcare is set to break barriers - piles of paper silos will transform into electronic silos, and data that was traditionally "fenced in" is "outsourced" to on-shore and/or off-shore business associates. This shift will require critical rethinking of "security across organization silos" where providers, beneficiaries, and business associated operate across IT silos with varying degrees of threat, vulnerability and risk exposure.

Cyber risks are associated with data at rest, data in flight and data in process. Each state of data requires different technologies and processes to enforce policies – e.g. encryption of data at rest to protect impermissible use of data, use of private-public keys to secure data in motion on the network, and measurable trustworthiness of the device and platform associated with the data in use.

The threats that must be addressed in the healthcare sector to protect data breaches at the various touch points may be broadly categorized as insider threats (authorized users, unpermitted use), device level infection, and network level compromise. The challenges in the healthcare ecosystem, therefore, include:

- Users: Administrators (Admission to Discharge), Physicians, Clinical Technicians, Nurses, Healthcare Workers & Assistants, Interns, Suppliers, Contractors

- Devices: Laptops, Desktops, Servers, Network Devices, Medical Devices, BYOD, Smartphones, Virtual Desktop Infrastructure, Virtual/Cloud Servers

- Networks: Remote Access (VPN), Wireless, Partner Access Networks (Business Associates, Insurance Providers, Pharmacies)

The workflow necessitates that electronic health records be protected from womb-to-tomb – from beneficiary to provider and business associates. The data therefore transits multiple IT silos, managed and unmanaged realms. This requires policies and processes to continuously monitor the healthcare ecosystem for detection of risks, indicators of a breach, and analysis of a security episode for remediation and breach notification to restore business operations to a trustworthy and normal posture.

The evolution of threats over the decade are clearly indicative of the diversity of methods, motives and means that hackers and cyber criminals use to conduct nefarious activities undetected. The attacks have evolved from social hacktivism, theft of intellectual property for financial gain, damage to critical assets or infrastructure, to ransomware (cyber blackmail). It is therefore critical for security stakeholders in the healthcare industry to take note and address the threats both as a technology innovation and process enhancement. The technologies of the past decade (Intrusion Detection Systems, Intrusion Prevention Systems, and Firewalls) have been reactive solutions aimed at malware detection, victim (system) analysis, malware (breach) analysis to derive well-known signatures to thwart repeat attacks. This does not solve the problem and only emboldens the cyber criminals to morph signatures and strike again without remorse.

Understanding how cyber-attacks are conceived, planned and executed with precision requires analogous approaches as in the healthcare profession – connecting biological markers to clinical symptoms. The DNA of a threat characterizes the behavior model and life cycle stages of malware across the controls evaded, devices infected, and network compromised. In intricate IT parlance, this translates to network dialog correlation, user-application-system action sequence correlation, and cognitive behavior recognition to analyze the evidence and identify the active risks that require counter measures as a treatment.

High Profile Breaches

The high-profile data breaches emphasize the need for CISOs to rethink both policy statements and enforcement processes within an Enterprises (small, medium and large) to address the dark side of the soft core – Residual Risk. An autopsy of breach analysis is likely to reveal a sequence of "blind spots" and "process oversights" that ought to cross-examine the technologies and processes that fail to provide the required resilience and indicators for effective and timely counter measures. Cyber-attacks succeed not because of any "willful neglect" or "careless attitudes" by C-level executives, economic decisions, network or system administrators, but because of "outmoded instrumentation" at the device and network level that is inadequate to provide "integrity markers". Cyber risks are associated with data at rest, data in flight and data in process. Each state of data requires different technologies and processes to enforce policies – e.g. encryption of data at rest to protect impermissible use of data, use of secure keys to protect data in motion on the network, and a metrics based operational integrity score for the device and platform associated with the data in use.

The threats that must be addressed to protect data breaches at the various touch points may be broadly categorized as insider threats (authorized users, unpermitted use), device level infection, and network level compromise. This requires policies and processes to continuously monitor the ecosystem for detection of risks, indicators of a breach, and analysis of a security episode for remediation and breach notification to restore business operations to a trustworthy and normal posture. Advanced threats leverage the privileges of authenticated and authorized users to gain access to data silos (network file shares, local file system) and access paths (VPN tunnel, remote access) to infect a system and take hold of the network for reconnaissance camouflaged in the maze of legitimate scans and outbound transactions (e.g. SSH, HTTP, FTP, DNS) that are difficult to introspect for reasonable intent. The data destruction motive of landed malware may be performed through low level driver interactions circumventing high level security controls.

Attacker attribution requires reliable information to analyze how the breach was orchestrated internally, identifying the origin of the malicious code (supply chain), and finally tracking down the location of the attackers. The warrant required in a breach investigation to convict the cyber criminals must provide credible evidence as assurance that no evasion techniques were detected, including use of Tor networks, Fast flux DNS, and IP address spoofing. Further, for long duration and high-volume data haul, determination of the corpus of actors by geo-location may be an authoritative assertion of the locality or distribution of the attackers.

Most investigations today that typically follow in the wake of high-profile breaches rely on static geo-location markers for the network addresses and domain names linked to the security episode. The availability of cloud computing services, elastic IPs, Tor networks coupled with the dynamic domain name services, domain name and IP address fast flux warrant evidence beyond reasonable doubt to determine true actors (perpetrators). Investigators must determine whether the attack was staged locally within the Enterprise, domestically within the country, internationally from a friendly nation or from rogue nations. This requires credible attribution of domain and IP address registration and anti-spoofing protection to rely on such evidence for inferences.

Breach Analysis includes contemporary methods to salvage forensic evidence from footprints on file systems and in non-volatile memory, and traceability for attribution of external actors (perpetrators and intermediaries leveraged to stage the attack). Tor networks pose a serious challenge because the network of virtual tunnels and relays provide anti-trace protection. The attacker could set preferred entry and exit nodes and also inform Tor which nodes to use. Attribution of IP addresses involved in activities linked to the delivery, command and control and data exfiltration merely identifies specific staging points. State actors may use Tor to deflect blame, or organized cyber criminals are likely to incriminate others by utilizing specific regional Tor entry and exit nodes. Whether data exfiltration was performed through a push or pull mechanism may provide credible evidence to ascertain whether a network of volunteer relays was used for anonymity.

Supply Chain Integrity is Key

Detecting infections at an endpoint device poses unique time and effort challenges for forensic analysis and incident response. These tasks are labor intensive and consume valuable human resources (IT, network, application, and system administrators). Remediation and recovery of an infected server may be accomplished expeditiously, through on-demand instantiation of a workload to restore operating capacity and reimaging the infected server from a controlled gold image respectively. However, end user workstations and devices require a meticulous evidence trail for soft recovery operations and incur asset downtime and work schedule disruption. A data breach casts a shadow of uncertainty on the integrity of multiple endpoints (managed workstations and servers, BYOD, mobile devices). Continuous integrity monitoring before a breach requires context and key indicators of risk that often remain hidden and undiscovered until after the breach. The runtime operational integrity is the key trust metric.

Undeniably, preemption is better than redemption. The status quo in multi-layer security is a "hard edge, soft core" mindset. A strategic and holistic defensive initiative requires a "resilient core", because cyber criminals target the core, not the edge, to take hold. The immune system at the endpoint requires a method to identify nefarious activities of applications that have "no innocent reason" to justify such actions. Protection controls are required to complement contemporary methods based on signatures, process introspection, heuristics, anomaly detection and machine learning – with platform instrumentation to enhance tamper resistance at the soft core, and localized real time analytics for active remediation before the breach. The solution provides decisive evidence in real time, to overcome reliance on indicators of compromise based on anchor biases and false positives. The false positives are due to expeditious decision logic that avoids missing information that lead to non-deterministic probabilities for predictions.

Perimeter Fallacy

The notion of a hardened edge as the security perimeter is a misconception. The soft core is the battleground. A plurality of systems and methods are necessary to design and build a holistic and resilient security architecture. Each security control provides a specific function – from detection to remediation. Controls that are complementary offer protections that are additive. A redundant security stack is key to avoid the cascade effect where one or more controls in the chain fail simultaneously during a data breach. The endpoint is the last line of defense. A data breach occurs not because of a single point of failure, but because of a series of failures. The subaddivity effect – the tendency to judge probability as a whole to be less than the probabilities of the parts – increases the residual risk that one is willing to take.

Signatures

Anti-Virus (AV) and Host based Intrusion Detection Systems (HIDS) rely on the availability of timely and reliable (zero-day) application reputation lists, file hash digests, persistent registry and file system footprints. This anchor bias on deny-lists poses a challenge as polymorphic variants easily circumvent such strategies that rely upon a corpus of honeypots deployed in the wild to harvest the metadata. However, use of signatures from reliable sources of threat intelligence is vital for efficient remediation of infected systems from discovered classes and families of malware.

Process Introspection

Process introspection-based approaches rely on well-known patterns of application execution profiles, associated registry and file system operations, on-the-fly observations through virtual execution in a sandbox (on the hypothesis that there is "one and only one" repetitive true behavior), memory footprints (dump, disassemble, and generate code call graphs), and non-volatile indicators crucial for the preservation of untainted evidence for forensic analysis. Obfuscation and volatile execution (traces erased) pose a major exploit that advanced malware leverage effectively against such a detection strategy. However, introspective methods provide valuable post discovery forensic insights for pattern generation.

Heuristics

Heuristic reasoning uses dictionary learning based on past observations, similarity indicators, probability metrics and shortcuts (computationally fast algorithms and approximations) and thereby avoids missing information and relies on one trait or piece of information. This anchor bias on traits leads to inaccuracies and false positives. However, heuristics offer valuable markers for predictive analysis.

Anomaly Detection

Anomaly based detection uses behavior baselining (with a temporal snapshot as the reference anchor) to measure deviation from the established baseline. This approach analyzes logs of activities (though malicious code does not generate trace logs), assesses scan harvests and applies restrictive reasoning with zero tolerance for entropy (though change is the only constant). Anomalous activities are not necessarily malicious behaviors, and an anomaly is not necessarily a risk or threat indicator. However, the "constant bias" is attuned with configuration and compliance management.

Machine Learning

Machine learning overlaps significantly with data mining for discovery and data-driven predictions or decisions. This approach facilitates pattern recognition, statistical learning, derivative context (for automated generation of rule grammar based on observation of discrete events), predictive reasoning, and intuitive decision logic. Such methods help automate the generation of inference-based threat intelligence to serve as inputs to sensors for enhanced detection.

Recommended Reading

Mocana Corporation	https://www.mocana.com
ISA/IEC 62443 Cybersecurity Certificate Programs	https://www.isa.org/training-and-certification/isa-certification/isa99iec-62443/isa99iec-62443-cybersecurity-certificate-programs
IIC Endpoint Security Best Practices	https://hub.iiconsortium.org/endpoint-security-best-practices
NIST Cybersecurity Framework	https://www.nist.gov/cyberframework
Trusted Computing Group	https://trustedcomputinggroup.org/
Federal Information Processing Standards	https://www.nist.gov/itl/publications-0/federal-information-processing-standards-fips
A Unified Vision for a Smarter Industry	https://www.fieldcommgroup.org/
NERC Reliability Standards	https://www.nerc.com/pa/Stand/Pages/ReliabilityStandards.aspx
ISO-31000 Risk Management	https://www.iso.org/iso-31000-risk-management.html
Foresight review of cyber security for the Industrial IoT	https://ocsiiot.web.ox.ac.uk/files/lrfforesightreviewofcybersecurityfortheiiotjuly2020pdf-0
FIDO Alliance	https://fidoalliance.org/
IoT SAFE	https://www.gsma.com/iot/iot-security/

Figures

Glossary

ACL	Access Control List
AMG	Anti-Malware Gateway
APM	Application Performance Management
ASIC	Application Specific Integrated Circuit
ATM	Asynchronous Transfer Mode
AV	Anti-Virus
BYOD	Bring Your Own Device
CAD	Computer Aided Design
CBM	Condition Based Monitoring (Maintenance)
CEO	Chief Executive Officer
CIO	Chief Information Officer
CIP	Critical Infrastructure Protection
CISO	Chief Information Security Officer
CRO	Chief Risk Officer
CTO	Chief Technology Officer
CVE	Common Vulnerabilities and Exposures
DHCP	Dynamic Host Configuration Protocol
DLP	Data Leakage Protection
DMZ	Demilitarized Zone
DNS	Domain Name System

ECU	Engine Control Unit
EHR	Electronic Health Record
EPHI	Electronic Protected Health Information
EPID	Enhanced Privacy ID
ESIM	Embedded SIM
FCG	Field Communications Group
FERC	Federal Energy Regulatory Commission
FIDO	Fast ID Online
FIPS	Federal Information Security Standards
FTP	File Transfer Protocol
HIDS	Host based Intrusion Detection System
HIPAA	Health Insurance Portability and Accountability Act
HITECH	Health Information Technology for Economic and Clinical Health Act
HMI	Human Machine Interface
HTTP	Hypertext Transmission Protocol
IaaS	Infrastructure as a Service
IDP	Intrusion Prevention System
IDS	Intrusion Detection System
IEC	International Electrotechnical Commission
IIC	Industrial Internet Consortium
IIoT	Industrial IoT
IIS	Internet Information Services
IKE	Internet Key Exchange
IoT	Internet of Things
IoT SAFE	IoT SIM Applet For Secure End-2-End Communication
IP	Internet Protocol
IPsec	Internet Protocol Security
ISA	International Society of Automation
ISIM	Integrated SIM
ISO	International Organization for Standardization
IT	Information Technology

LAN	Local Area Network
LOB	Line of Business
MEC	Multi-Access Edge Computing
MSSP	Managed Security Services Provider
NAC	Network Admission (Access) Control
NAT	Network Address Translation
NERC	North American Electric Reliability Corporation
NGFW	Next Generation Firewall
NIST	National Institute of Standards and Technology
NOC	Network Operations Center
ODM	Original Device Manufacturer
OEM	Original Equipment Manufacturer
OT	Operational Technology
PaaS	Platform as a Service
PKI	Public Key Infrastructure
PSK	Pre-Shared Key
RBAC	Role Based Access Control
RTOS	Real Time Operating System
SaaS	Software as a Service
SCADA	Supervisory Control and Data Acquisition
SCAP	Security Content Automation Protocol
SIEM	Security Information and Event Management
SIM	Subscriber Identification Module
SMTP	Simple Mail Transfer Protocol
SOAR	Security Orchestration, Automation and Response
SOC	Security Operations Center
SSH	Secure Shell
SSL	Secure Sockets Layer
STIG	Security Technical Implementation Guide
STIX	Structured Threat Information eXpression
TAXII	Trusted Automated eXchange of Intelligence Information

TCP	Transmission Control Protocol
TCU	Telematics Control Unit
TLS	Transport Layer Security
TPM	Trusted Platform Module
UAV	Unmanned Aerial Vehicle
UDP	User Datagram Protocol
VLAN	Virtual LAN
VPN	Virtual Private Network
WAN	Wide Area Network
WINS	Windows Internet Name Server

Epilogue

The purpose of this rendition was to provide professionals in the infinite field of cybersecurity and emerging data sciences a microscopic and telescopic view to reflect on the past, contemplate deeper on the present, and look farther for course correction in the future. Rapid advances in science and technology often cause consequential retrogressions in status quo and unintended consequences to humanity and the planet. Disruptive innovation sometimes causes inadvertent harm to society and future generations. The several decades of technical and business knowhow harvested while working on innovative solutions in the field of embedded systems, telecommunications, network and cyber security at large corporations and Silicon Valley startups have convinced me that this dream is an eternal pursuit. While investors are focused on return on investment, value creation will always demand the return of innovation by steadfast professionals.

If one was to analyze the subconscious daily dreams of billions of human minds on this planet today, it would undoubtedly be an enormous challenge in human psychology. Analyzing the minds of billions of devices with artificial intelligence and machine learning will pose a parallel conundrum in digital psychology.

For investors, entrepreneurs, students, and creators of the future, the journey is just beginning.

About the Author

Chief Technology and Product Officer, Mocana Corporation

Srinivas Kumar has more than 30 years of hands-on engineering and management experience in computer networking and security.

Prior to joining Mocana, he was the CTO of TaaSera. He founded TaaSware in 2011 (acquired by TaaSera in 2012). During his time at TaaSware he served as an entrepreneur-in-residence at SRI International. Prior to that, he was a solutions architect in the networking and security business unit at VMware. He was previously the VP of engineering and solutions architect for identity-based access controls at Applied Identity, until it was acquired by Citrix. He has served in senior project and architect roles at Nortel, Lucent and TranSwitch. Earlier in his career, as engineering manager at Firearms Training

Systems (acquired by Meggitt Training Systems), he led the design and development of real time marksmanship and squad engagement simulators for training law enforcement personnel and the military.

He holds 28 U.S. patents in the field of cyber-protection for IoT, cybersecurity, user and application identity-based access controls, network and endpoint security, and evidence based predictive analytics. He has led engineering efforts to certify products for common criteria, FIPS, DO-178, US DoD and NATO standards. He holds a BE degree in electrical engineering from Bombay University, and an MS degree in electrical and computer engineering from Clemson University.

https://www.linkedin.com/in/srinivas-kumar-2634a1/